# 5,742 Days

A mother's journey through loss

## ANNE-MARIE COCKBURN

infiniteideas

First published in 2013 by
Infinite Ideas Limited
36 St Giles
Oxford
OX1 3LD
United Kingdom
www.infideas.com

A CIP catalogue record for this book is available from the British Library
ISBN 978–1–908984–24–1

Cover designed by Bigtop Design Ltd
Text designed and typeset by GRID
Printed in Britain by 4edge Ltd, Essex

*To my little twig, Martha*

# Acknowledgements

I'd like to thank everyone who has helped play a crucial part in my recovery over the past few months. So many people have shown so much compassion and concern as to my wellbeing at the loss of my dear Martha and many of you have exclaimed that the city of Oxford, in which she was born and raised, feels that loss too. It takes a village to raise a child and it is with that sentiment that I raised Martha – she was our child and her death affected so many of us, but that same village now supports and comforts me and for that I am incredibly grateful.

Martha's friends have played an enormous part in my healing and I am delighted that, despite Martha's absence, they are still happy to feature in my new life.

My wonderful family have tirelessly comforted and cared for me during my darkest hours – enabling me to see the light again. Thank you – I love you all so dearly.

# Introduction

On 20th July 2013 my daughter, Martha Fernback, died, aged fifteen. This is my story, from the minute an unrecognised number appeared on my mobile phone screen and a stranger's voice told me that my daughter was gravely ill and they were trying to save her life. Martha had taken half a gram of white powder which turned out to be MDMA (ecstasy). It was an innocent mistake.

This book relates my journey since that moment. It's in real time, as writing has helped me to cope during the times when everything became too much. The pain was so immense that I had to channel it somewhere to get it out of my system; I did this by writing my way through the agony.

Martha was my only child and I am a single parent.

# Sunday 21st July: Day 1

My fifteen-year-old daughter died yesterday. I watched them try to save her. They pumped her chest and drilled something into her shin, but I knew she was already dead on arrival at the John Radcliffe Hospital in Oxford. They elevated her arms, but I don't know why, her eyes were half open and she was way beyond the clouds and stars already.

I was calling to her in the same tone I last heard when I gave birth to her. A tone so unearthly and raw that it haunted the entire corridor of medical staff. Two nurses stood by me, I restlessly laid my head on one and squeezed their hands as I yearned for my girl to come back to me. I needed the love of strangers and it was there in abundance.

I couldn't breathe once they announced what I already knew, my fingers and toes were tingling. They put me on a wheeled chair and asked me what I wanted to do. What do I want to do? I don't know what to do – what do you do in a situation like this?

Strangely though, I didn't want to be with her, I didn't feel a connection. I felt strongly that she left before she even arrived at the hospital. I didn't want to hold her – I just needed to get out of that room.

They wheeled me into a side room and I sat up on a bed. They gave me a cup of sugary tea – I can still remember that tea, it was like drinking the world, and everything in it was good, and kind, and wholesome again.

My parents arrived and I heard them outside the curtain. They gave them the bad news and then unveiled me from behind the curtain as though I was a curiosity. Their faces were mosaic floors, their stoop said that life would never be the same again for any of us. They were devastated, but I sensed they knew they needed to give what little they had left to me, before allowing their own feelings to surface.

The police and various official people needed to speak to us. The CID guy spoke to us and I watched his lips move through the fog of my mind. He set out procedures and timelines to help us understand what to expect over the coming days. Martha was now the property of the coroners until their investigations and toxicology tests were carried out. She'd hopefully be released to us within a couple of days, which meant she could be moved to the hospital mortuary and we'd be able to see her again.

It was very clear to me that I needed to donate any of her organs that could possibly be saved, but the autopsy, toxicology tests, etc., meant that they were limited as there wasn't enough time. But I was told we could donate a valve from her heart which we agreed to do.

My friends started to arrive, all trying to dilute my pain and carry my burden for themselves. Never have so many people in one day told me they loved me. Colleagues and friends all declaring they care for me and that they'll do whatever I need.

My life goes on from here. The wheels keep turning, they need to, and, although my heart is smashed into a million pieces, slowly with all this support and nurturing, I can be glued back together again.

# Monday 22nd July: Day 2

My eyelids finally stopped fighting the sleep last night and I slept deeply and soundly. I wake up early. My heart is beating, but it pangs with the loss, knowing that I will always miss her. I missed her even when she was only away for a few hours, but this type of 'missing' is peculiar, unnatural. Getting used to her not being here goes against what every cell in my body feels. I am a mother, that is what I do.

Mothers care and plan ahead, mothers nurture and nag you to tidy your bedroom. Mothers tell you to shower after you've been swimming in the lake. Martha would make excuses and go to bed with the grit of the day on her. I'll never get to nag her again, I'll never get to tell her that her room is a mess ... oh how I wish I could nag her again and hear her excuses ... "I'll do it later, I'll shower after kayaking tomorrow". I'd be both bemused and irritated by this, but that is a luxury now that I'll never get to practise again. I am still a mother, but not a practising one. I have all these mothering skills, which I know will always be useful in my life, but their original purpose is no longer what they'll be used for.

So I did what I needed to do today. I went online and started looking at coffins: what would she like, what would Martha choose? She was far from traditional but she wouldn't want anything gimmicky either. The answers come to me gently. I know that whatever is chosen, it'll be lovely and really, does it matter that much? The true meaning of life has hit me like a bolt of lightning and the previous version of me now seems trivial – but it's tragic that this had to happen in order for this stoic version of myself to surface.

I'm going through her clothes today, to choose an outfit to dress her in. She liked to wear crop tops and denim shorts that were more revealing than any parent is comfortable with. "Pull those shorts down", I hear the previous version of myself say. Today I say, "Martha, what would you like me to dress you in – what outfit is the right one to represent you for the very last time?" It definitely won't be denim shorts and a crop top, but it'll be something that'll show my precious daughter off beautifully.

Martha, if you are with me now, please hold my hand and guide me to show me what you want. I love you so much and don't know where to channel this love now. I have too much of it and it was *all* for you. I'll give some to myself now as I need it; I'll give some to family, friends and strangers, but I've still got too much left. It feels like a burden, but I know it'll get easier.

I came home today, as I wanted to be in the tranquillity of my home to try to gather my thoughts. The sun was streaming through the rooms as I looked around at the array of things in my life which were important until two days ago.

I opened a pile of condolence cards, double-blinking, trying hard to take the words in and decipher the names at the end. People were reaching out to me and holding my hand via ink and paper; wanting to express their feelings in order to ease my pain. Their offers of help and outpourings proclaimed how much they thought of Martha.

I wander around the rooms and go upstairs into her bedroom. I look out of her window and up at the sky. I take a slow, deep breath and wander back out.

My phone buzzes and rings all day long; the distraction is welcome. I have a long telephone interview to discuss the donation of Martha's heart valves, which will be kept in liquid nitrogen until they're needed. It's comforting to think that one day Martha's heart valves will be pumping blood around another body – connecting her with life again.

Close friends arrive and help tidy up a bit. It's hot outside and feels stuffy. I need to get out in the breeze, so we take pizza to Port Meadow, along with a framed photo of Martha, and sit by the river. I lie on the ground and look up at the sky; are you there, Martha? Show me a sign. A storm brews in the distance and we welcome the breeze, rain and lightning that it brings. It feels exhilarating to be soaked and to not care.

We go the Wolvercote Cemetery and look around. The gravestones alarm me, the names and dates, as the realisation dawns on me. I hadn't considered that, but then why would I? We wander around the woodland area and rabbits run around. It doesn't feel right. I don't like this. I spot a newly dug grave out of the corner of my eye and look away from it quickly.

We head over to visit a good friend I've known for years, who lost her husband two years ago. She's wise and knowledgeable and it reassures me to hear her valuable advice. This is the end of the second day without my girl. I used to think there weren't enough hours in the day; now I think there are too many.

# Tuesday 23rd July: Day 3

It's 5.12am. I listen to the silence of my home. My eyes sting as I went to bed at 12.45am and now find myself stirring to bring myself reluctantly into this new day. I come downstairs and reach for my laptop. Writing is like oxygen to me right now, it always has been throughout my life, but this agony has taken away the self-conscious filter that has built up over the years. I left any insecurities and ego on the floor of the emergency department at the hospital. All that is left is pure and unpretentious as though I've died and been reborn – no longer am I affected by social norms or shaped by life experiences that tell me how I should behave.

Everything is suddenly clear to me, my natural views and opinions are all now motivated by love and compassion. There is no anger inside me, I'm full of pure light and peace. The pain is there and sits at the pit of my stomach, but something is gently guiding me forward and that feels comforting.

The clock on the wall ticks loudly and my heart beats along with it, reminding me that life exists and time goes on regardless. I feel empty and restless inside my entire being. My starving stomach gurgles and I am glad of this as it helps me to feel something at least. I look at Martha's beautiful smiling photograph on the mantelpiece and smile back at her. Her mesmerising eyes take me to another world as they always did. I never tired of gazing at her face; she knew this and would say, "Are you admiring your work?" and I'd laugh a deep guttural laugh. She'd then tell me her face was copyrighted and that would make me laugh again.

With this new day I can only keep looking up to the light and breathing it in to the depths of my soul. It recharges me and envelops me, providing some comfort. I just need to 'be'; what else can I do right now? So I float along and allow the universe to show me the way – she knows what I need and so I follow her peacefully.

I showered and got ready, and that was when I received the news that the post mortem operation carried out yesterday was inconclusive at this stage and that further tests would need to be carried out over the coming weeks. I was advised that Martha's brain had been completely removed as part of the autopsy – this news horrified me and I felt angry and distraught. I was too fragile to hear this. I wondered whether they'd shaved off all her lovely hair. We were also told that we needed to decide whether to hold up the funeral and bury her without her brain, or if we'd like to donate her brain for medical science at a later date.

# Wednesday 24th July: Day 4

A friend brought over coffee and a croissant for me very early this morning. We talked for hours about Martha's quirky little ways and we laughed and cried about the things she said and did.

Martha's dad arrived from abroad. It was odd to see him under these circumstances. I took him to Martha's bedroom and showed him the little bits and pieces that she kept around her. A pack of Uno cards by her bed, glowing plastic stars on her ceiling, Buffy, the teddy he bought for her when she was a toddler and which she cherished. He sat on her bed and I sat on the floor; we chatted about how we both were feeling and tried to console one another.

We then went to the tribute tree near where Martha collapsed. The flowers were a stunning array of colours, set out as though a fairy wand had placed them there. The lake and pontoon looked idyllic; it was obvious why she loved coming here so regularly. We sat on the bench and read through the condolence notes, sniffing our tears away whilst reading the words of her young friends through blurry, tear-strewn eyes. I tried to sense her presence: "Are you here my darling girl?" I looked around at the ground, knowing that her final breath had passed her beautiful lips here.

## Wednesday 24th July: Day 4

The next part of the day loomed over us and sent chills through my already aching stomach – we had an appointment to view Martha's body at the Coroner's Office. We stopped off at a café to force ourselves to eat a little something. I watched the people in the café as though they were moving in slow motion, going about their daily lives. Viewing what ordinary life looks like from our very extraordinary haze.

At the hospital we were briefed, taken through all the formalities of what to expect and given an update on where things were at present. We were led into a very warm circular room which had a sunny, domed ceiling. Martha lay in the middle ready for us. Her hair was intact and her pallor was different from how she looked on Saturday, a slight pink hue had returned which was more pleasant than the yellow and grey complexion I witnessed before.

I told her that Mum and Dad were here for her and gently stroked her hair. I gazed longingly at her face and wondered why this had happened. She was stone cold, but her forehead was clammy. I felt nothing. I left Martha's dad to have a moment with her alone.

We visited a funeral director and met a lady who helped us go over the various options available. So much to take in; how are grief-stricken people supposed to deal with all this formality?

I feel far away from Martha today, but I'm coping as I have no choice but to start to build a new life for myself. Oh how I dread the milestones, the 'how old would she be now?' thoughts. I'll never have another child, I put everything into her life and, thinking about it, she lived a full and abundant life in fifteen years.

# Thursday 25th July: Day 5

I lay on my parents' garden swing and watched a bumble bee walk amongst the blades of grass, climbing over dead leaves and zigzagging along. What are you looking for? Are you looking for pollen? I'm suddenly reminded of a conversation I had with Martha the other day about the fact that food prices are rising and that supplies will be in jeopardy as tens of thousands of bees died in America recently. It's going to be a real problem in the future.

I had one ear on her as my eyes scanned the supermarket; my mind was a shopping list of dinner and other bits needed to feed my girl. She said that future generations may need to live on protein. At the time I thought what a fascinating little character she was; would I have thought that thought as a teenager – would I have been bothered about the depletion of the bumble bee population and rising food prices? She was an incredibly gripping storyteller, eloquent and knowledgeable.

I follow the bumble bee around the garden: are you looking for pollen? Should I take a flower to you and put it in your path? I don't, as I also understand that there is an order to nature. It's cruel sometimes and captivating at others.

# Saturday 27th July: Day 7

Precisely one week ago to the minute, an unrecognised number appeared on my mobile phone screen and a stranger's voice said, "Your daughter is gravely ill and we're trying to save her." I didn't really understand at first as I thought, oh she's probably got a vomiting bug from swimming in the lake. Gravely ... Now, I know exactly what that word means, but I rejected its meaning, the immediate shock stopping me from accepting it.

A friend's husband collected me and drove me to A&E as the emergency team on site had advised me to go there, rather than to where Martha was, as the emergency services would bring her straight to the hospital. Two little boys were in the back of the car, one was singing innocently. His dad tried to shush him as I made my emergency phone calls, but I didn't mind his sweet innocence and turned to smile at his beautiful little face through my shock. I couldn't get in touch with anyone as all their phones rang out.

I arrived at the A&E reception shaking as though I was frozen. I explained what was going on and was taken round to see the emergency team. They looked on their system and couldn't see anything registered yet. I called the stranger back. She was still with Martha and updated me with what was going on, helping me to explain to the emergency team what was unfolding.

Their demeanour suddenly changed and I knew that they now realised how serious this was as I mentioned the helicopter had been called and couldn't land due to the position of the lake in relation to where Martha was. There was talk of driving Martha in the ambulance to the helicopter, but nothing was certain at this stage.

I was taken to the family room which was air conditioned and austere. I hated being alone in there. I sat down rocking myself back and forth and put my face in my hands, wailing. I kept saying, "Please save my girl, please, please, keep her safe." I couldn't stay in that room, I needed daylight, I couldn't get a signal on my phone and I needed to alert my family. The staff informed me that I wouldn't get a signal in there as the walls are lined with lead. I went outside and kept trying to get through to my parents but there was no answer from their home phone or mobiles. I kept trying, but again, there was no answer. Eventually they called me back and I was able to tell them to come straight to the John Radcliffe Hospital.

A week ago, exactly, during the time I am writing this, the sun fell out of the sky and boomed down onto the earth and The Register that tallies the human race clicked -1 as her beautiful life slipped away.

I felt as though it had clicked -2 and that I had gone with her. Instead I was wrapped in a hazy cocoon; I became a newborn baby who was reliant on everyone for everything. I needed water to be poured into my mouth, I needed to be held, rocked and patted when I cried to make me feel better. I needed wrapping in a blanket, my bath to be run for me and my clothes laid out by my loving family. I needed help to walk again.

This past week has been like a crazy French movie, beautiful, peculiar, thought-provoking, poignant, confusing and refreshingly authentic. My insides are awash with the rhythm of life, but my eyes are daydreaming and my body seems like a pointless vehicle transporting the pain inside me.

I lay in the bath the other night and looked down at the pulse in my groin, my stomach also twitching with the same little gentle rhythm, sending ripples out to the surface of the bathwater. Martha's life was like that, she sent ripples out through everyone who ever met her, reaching around the world and living on forever in the tide.

The sun rises the next day, albeit bruised. I'm watered by my loving family and the sunlight gives me strength and helps me to grow again.

# Wednesday 31 July: Day 11

So today I'm back in my lovely home. I've floated through the past few days numb, and without any concept of time. Four hours pass and I'm convinced it's only five minutes. I feel peculiar because I haven't emotionally broken down for days and seem to be a little too in control of my emotions.

I know that all feelings are appropriate at times like this, but when I'm doing normal things, the routine seems like I'm being disloyal to my grief and to Martha. I'm not suppressing anything, as I know if I do that it'll only resurface later and I'll need to deal with it then. So this is my new version of normal and it is totally natural, for the moment anyway.

The washing machine still contains laundry from our idyllic last day at the beach, the day before she died. She had been complaining of having swollen glands and was exhausted from weeks of studying for her exams, so I thought as it was Friday I'd let her rest and phoned her school and told them she wasn't feeling well.

Luckily a friend had lent us their VW van a few days previously as we had to empty out a garage we rented. I picked up Martha's boyfriend and we were on Sandbanks beach by 9am. I looked around at the vast deserted beach and walked along to decide

where to place our towels. I found a spot, staking out our
territory for the day. I plonked myself down and panned left to
right over the misty distant landscape. The sea was glistening,
the seagulls were dancing majestically in the sky and I slowly
breathed in the beautiful day ahead. This was perfect, it was just
what we needed.

Martha immediately wanted to be buried in the sand; she lay
there as her boyfriend scooped up handfuls and patted them
around her. I watched them, bemused, and felt carefree and
tranquil. Cocooned in sand, she smiled and laid her head back
as her boyfriend made her a sandy pillow. A toddler passed by in
his dad's arms and his dad said, "Look it's a head in the sand with
no body." The toddler stared, his brain trying to understand what
this meant.

It was now Martha's boyfriend's turn to be buried, so she got busy
pushing piles of sand around him, repeatedly placing handfuls

on toes which kept poking through. Being Martha she then decided to give him boobs, using shells for nipples. I told her the breasts were too low and that he wasn't a middle-aged woman; he looked down and agreed and she slid them a few inches higher. We took photos and laughed at the silliness of it all, British culture at its best. Quaint and peculiar.

The man and toddler passed by again and the man said "Look, the head has changed, how did that happen?" The toddler stared again and grinned as he understood the joke.

We then heard the song 'O Sole Mio', which most British people associate with the 'Just One Cornetto' advert. I looked around to see where it was coming from and realised it was from a gondola-style boat approaching the shoreline. I handed £10 to Martha and asked her to get us all an ice-cream, as how could we resist. The boat was like an oasis on the water; people queued standing in knee-high water, and I chuckled to myself at the novelty of it all as I watched them waiting, while the music lingered in the air.

Martha and her boyfriend went off and played in the water with a ball we had brought with us. I glanced up at them now and again and felt so proud at how grown up they were. At one point Martha sat at the edge of the water as her boyfriend played with the ball by himself – she wasn't glancing at him for approval or looking over to see what he was doing, she was sitting contentedly in the sand.

As they made their way back to me, I watched them approach. Martha was wearing his t-shirt which went almost down to her knees. They sat down next to me and I suggested we get some food from the kiosk behind us, so we got some cod goujons and chips served in cones and shared them as we sat on our towels.

As we drove back from that trip we listened to the soundtrack to *The Lion King*. I remember at one point I was holding Martha's right hand and her boyfriend was holding her left and she said, "I feel so loved right now." I asked her boyfriend to describe her in one word and he said "quirky", which I agreed with. We all laughed at that and sang along to the music as the miles sped behind us.

I get a pang when I think about doing her laundry and then what? It's a precipitous moment, when I can choose to either jump from real life into the past, escape in my head to the spirit world to try to connect with her or just be in the now, agonising as it is.

I live a combination of all of these lives, visiting them when the moment feels right. I look back and wonder, memories and moments slipping through my mind like old film reels. My fear of the future and what that will consist of and the pain in my heart which stops me from becoming desensitised, remind me that this is real; it's hideous and terrible.

# Saturday 3rd August: Day 14

I lay in bed avoiding getting up, I'm constantly exhausted, but don't want to slip into a serious depression, so I text a few friends and make plans for the day ahead. The sunlight peeps from below the blind and I close my eyes to try to connect with my girl. I tell her I miss her, but I'm numb and feel nothing as the sedatives that are holding me together stop me from feeling too much.

I come downstairs and look out at the street. People peer into shop windows, a car door slams, a lady cycles to the post box and leans over on her bike, reaching forward to pop a white envelope in. I wonder what's in that letter; is it to a lonely elderly friend, or perhaps it's a birthday card congratulating somebody on making it through another year! Is it destined to land on an exotic doorstep, arriving slightly warped, affected by the long journey and humidity. Or is it just a bill being paid the old-fashioned way?

I watch people watching people, I always have done – the girl who observes. The girl who describes herself as a sociable recluse. But in light of what's happened, I now know that although I'm very comfortable in my own company, I love being surrounded by people, just preferring small intimate groups to large ones.

## Saturday 3rd August: Day 14

I recognise the voice of a friend outside on the street. "Bye love", I hear her say in her northern accent. I know this community so well that I don't even need to look out and check to know that it's her. I peep across the road and see her bag outside her shop. The layers of wallpaper of my life, my history over the decades is ten layers deep, my new life being pasted on top of the last layer.

The lovely friends who hosted a barbecue for me last night wander along the street. The sun beats down on them and the mild summer breeze makes their clothing and hair dance. As they chopped, marinated and prepared the food I felt we were on their minds: Martha's lovely spirit glistened in the salad dressing, her ethereal giggle was in every little golden orb of the corn on the cob.

Every bite of food they made was medicinal, to help nurture me back to life. It was delicious and with every bite I felt their love and tenderness energise and heal me. They were gentle, tender and in disbelief. It must be peculiar for people to observe someone like me during times like this. I'd hate to be my audience right now, I'm being very chatty and normal as I give them information about what's been going on.

I provide them with matter-of-fact, stomach-churning conversation as though I'm discussing the weather. My friends listen to me intently – does it help them to try to make sense of what's happened, perhaps? But it's not about that. What's happened doesn't make sense and nothing will bring her back, but we talk through our grief surrounded by the people we trust, who want to do what they can to help. From my dry eyes I see tears at the edges of theirs; I'm desensitised because the most recent chapter in my life has punched me below the belt and I'm still winded from the shock.

I don't feel self-conscious about imposing this topic on them. My intuition tells me all I need to know right now and I listen intently to it. I've never been very good at putting myself first and living life for myself, but that's fine as I get a lot of satisfaction out of helping other people. It's a welcome distraction, but I know now that there must be something left for me too and I won't lose sight of that.

Everyone says that Oxford has stopped and that they can't think or talk about anything else. If only Martha knew how far she reached and how many lives she touched. It's like the film *It's a Wonderful Life*, which Martha and I watched every Christmas Eve: one life reaches so so far and impacts so much. 'George Bailey, please lasso the moon and bring her back to me', I plead. I know this isn't possible, so I'll dance by the light of the moon instead.

I picture a Christmas tree and the final scene from that film, the little girl saying, "Every time a bell rings an angel gets his wings". I'll allow the people of my community to come to my home bearing gifts to show that they love me and perhaps I'll meet my George Bailey one day and he can lasso the moon for me.

A friend just texted me a photo of her sister's twins, born late last night. I have tears of joy in my eyes. The cycle of life. Hatches, matches and despatches.

# Sunday 4th August: Day 15

I'm feeling it today. I decided to take two sedatives yesterday instead of four as I felt that being numb was inappropriate and stopping me from allowing my emotions to flow freely. So I got up early today and immediately felt discontented and emotional; the clarity I thought I needed is now an unwelcome guest and I want to revoke the invitation and return to my comfortably numb state.

My friends take me for an early morning walk to Port Meadow, which I had agreed to, but each step is like the ascent of Mount Everest and the previous spring in my step is now a reluctant drag of my feet through the gravel, almost teenage-like; stroppy and ungrateful.

The last time I walked this route was with my girl after dinner one sunny night. Martha finds a weed and sticks it to my back. I then pretend to yawn and put an arm over her shoulder, "Love you darling", I say, whilst sneakily patting the weed to the back of her top. "Have you stuck it to my back?" she demands. "No," I say, "I dropped it back on the towpath by the canal." I hold my palms up to prove my innocence and as she walks ahead, I take a photo of the weed stuck to her back.

When we reach Port Meadow she borrows my phone to take some 'selfies' with me 'photo bombing' in the background. I tell her to flick back to the previous photo, which unveils the picture of the weed stuck to the back of her top. She laughs and tries to remove it, struggling to reach it. I laugh and run away as she tries to stick it to my back again.

But today, I'm not with my girl and we're never going to walk this route together ever again. Her absence and that realisation feels like someone has touched a lit a match to my insides and the embers are slowly igniting my organs one by one. But the pain doesn't bother me.

## Sunday 4th August: Day 15

Never seeing her beautiful face again bothers me, never walking this journey with her sticking that silly little weed to my back bothers me, never hearing her incredible baby-like giggle bothers me. Never ever sharing another moment for the rest of my entire life with her bothers me. My incinerated insides don't bother me whatsoever. They can burn an inferno up and beyond the atmosphere and down to the earth's core for all I care. All material possessions could be thrown on the bonfire this inferno creates and I wouldn't shed one tear of regret.

Just bring back her beating heart and let me hold it in the palm of my hands, let me feel its warmth and be comforted by its natural rhythm. Let me inhale the earthy irony smell of blood and rejoice that she's back in the safety of my arms.

So I reluctantly make my descent to Port Meadow with my friends. The wild horses, one with her foal right by her side, cows chewing grass, early morning dogwalkers and geese all provide a perfectly pleasant scene, which I would have previously found mesmerising. But today it provides me with no solace and I stand there with my arms folded, fatigue and memories of the previous visit eating away at me, and my heart misses a beat. I turn for home and leave Port Meadow behind me. Will I ever find solace? I do hope so as with every beat my own heart makes, it reminds me that hers never will again.

## Monday 5th August: Day 16

I rummage through a drawer and open a box containing a pile of cards, the top one declaring, 'It's a Girl'. I notice a pink ankle tag and pick it up; the hand writing says 'Girl of Anne-Marie Cockburn Born: 30.10.97, 06.41am'. The ankle tag had been baggy on her minuscule ankle, as despite being five days overdue, she was only 5lb 4oz.

I inspect the tiny tag and slide it onto two of my fingers; it fits snugly. This tag marked the very beginning of my journey as a mother. How far we've come since then, little Martha, and what an incredible journey it's been – an absolute adventure. My head is a kaleidoscope of memories, all piled up, and I'm trying to find a use for them all now. They will always be relevant, but how can I do them justice? How can I possibly provide an accurate account of it all and bring the essence of her character to life? Am I trying to bring her back to life, perhaps, but then, who could blame me?

I glance up and realise I am encircled by sympathy cards from many of the same people who, fifteen years ago, were congratulating me; one big bittersweet cardboard hug. As I read each card I can feel the emotion of the person writing to me, how they felt and their concern in ensuring that they said the right thing. What do you say to a single mother who has lost her only child? As I read their heartfelt words, each card and envelope seeps with the emotion of the person who sent it, permeating my fingertips and pouring out in my own tears before plopping back onto their handwriting.

It all seems so neat, the circle of life; one box of 'congratulations' cards and an imminent box of 'condolence' cards. To be honest, it's the bit beyond all this I'm dreading, when the cards come down and 'normal' life tries to find its place in my new obscure schedule. I visualise 'normal' cautiously floating to the surfacing and saying, "Are you ready yet?" I give a derisory glance and 'normal' sinks swiftly back into my subconscious to surface at a later date.

The strange thing about bereavement is that I have no idea when this fatigue will leave me and I will regain my strength. It takes as long as it takes and in the meantime, I drag my friends and family along with me. I'm mindful that there must come a point when I will need to 'change the record' and start to accept it, but at the moment, it's a bit like letting go of oxygen — I need to keep her spirit alive and feel the essence of her character.

On 5th June she finally got her braces removed from her teeth. Every six weeks over eighteen months, we trundled on the bus to the orthodontist for checkups. She was so happy, running her tongue over her lovely smooth and straight teeth. She said she felt as though she had phantom leg syndrome and we all laughed at this description, which was so typical of her humour. So now I feel as though I've got phantom Martha syndrome and probably always will have. She'll always be beside me holding my hand.

# Wednesday 7th August: Day 18

I've never been away from my girl for more than a fortnight at a time and it's now nineteen days since I last saw her alive. The finality of knowing that I'll never see her again is agonising. I look up the word agony in the dictionary and it says 'intense pain or mental suffering, severe struggle.' Yes, I agree, but it's the not knowing how long the agony will last that's the main problem. The sunset last night was mesmerising, the sun descending onto a duvet of intense peachy red hues. Every dusk for me indicates one day further from when my girl was last with me, alive and well.

But I mustn't let my heart sink with the sunset at every dusk, nor groan with dread at every dawn. I'm trying so hard to remain mentally healthy and to welcome in each new day, but it takes so much courage and motivation for me to travel this uncharted route. Even my spontaneous nature is finding this adventure one step too far – I want to go onto TripAdvisor and give it a zero rating. Don't ever come here, I don't recommend it to anyone.

That said, I'm getting the best side of every human being who knows me. It's like the entire community has had a committee meeting, agenda set, minutes noted and action points agreed. Right, you take round scones and cream, I'll fill her freezer, you're on coffee duty and you guys look after her wheelie bins; let's book her some reflexology and a massage too. I'll do her nails, you do lunch duty tomorrow.

Astounding, utterly incredible, all this love and care pouring into me, lifting me off the floor I want to cling to and never move from. There is no set way to rebuild a bereft human being, as we're all unique, but all of our basic needs are exactly the same: we all need food, water and love. That is it, pure and simple.

# Thursday 8th August: Day 19

I have lots of meetings today. I sit up in bed and swing my legs over the edge, planting the balls of my feet on the floor. I reach over and pull up the blind. I thought I heard rain, but there is a beautiful morning unfolding; I ask whoever is listening to help me. I'm emotional today – there are tears waiting, building up pressure behind the dam of my medication. My demeanour is lacklustre. I shower, as that's what you do every day. I curl my eyelashes and wonder why. A female ritual, but it's just what we do – it seems so pointless to me now, but I do it anyway as it represents some form of normality and there is comfort in that.

I sit on the bench at the bus stop feeling lonely; Martha would normally be by my side at this bus stop. A friend comes up and sits with me, asking me how I am and the tears start to flow from my bewildered eyes. I am honest with my friend as I know it's terribly sad and tragic, but at the core of me I also feel determined and strong and know that I'll find my way through this. It is what it is and I'm not going to pretend, there is no room for fakery in my life.

As the bus floats me into the city centre everything spins past the window like reels; my senses are so heightened at the moment, I'm noticing so much. Snippets of conversations, smells wafting past from food outlets, colourful clothing all flash past me from the crowds of people walking intently whilst I meander. My shoulders are stooped and each step is slow, yet definite, a daydream of a daydream. I sigh as there are so many memories of my little ghost and me in this city centre, her favourite shops and the miles we must have walked on these pavements together over the past fifteen years.

When I get home I notice an envelope on my doormat and know what it is even before I've opened it. I take a deep breath, the Arctic Monkeys tickets I ordered a few weeks ago for her sixteenth birthday on 30th October have arrived. I was really looking forward to her being sixteen; she was turning into such a stunning young woman.

# Saturday 10th August: Day 21

Three weeks in, having pot holed my way down to the depths of this abyss, I'm absolutely perplexed as to how I navigate my way back to the surface. My internal sat nav has led me off-track into no-man's-land; I'm pressing 'reset' but the screen is stuck. An SOS has been sent out and swarms of hands are reaching down to help pull me out, but unless I take the first step, nobody can get to me. There is a serpent in my stomach eating me from the inside out and it gnaws greedily, draining me of the vital energy I need to take that one step back to safety.

For the past three weeks I've been repeating a reassuring mantra to try to convince myself and everyone around me: 'I'm strong, I know I've still got a life and a future and I'll get through this', but she's really not coming back to me is she? There is no hope of that, so how do I do this? When do I start to find pleasure again in my current life? So despite the affirmations of the mantra, I don't believe a single word of it now. My fingers have been blocking my ears from hearing the mantra as I know if I start to believe it then I get to 'normal' and I don't want to do normal without her. Simple as that, I do NOT want to DO IT without her!

Martha's eyes are everywhere I glance and she's saying, "Mum, carry on without me, I'm fine", but I want to grab her and feel her warm cheek next to mine again, I want her to lay her head on my shoulder and stand chest to chest, heartbeat to heartbeat, just like we did the minute she was born, when I laid my tiny Martha on my chest and our hearts beat together.

I know it's selfish of me to want this as all the people who love me don't want to see me suffer as I am, and the thoughts in my head today are preventing me from starting my journey of healing.

Over the past twenty-one days I've cried enough tears to water all the seeds in Africa, to provide nourishment to dying children. But moving away from romantic, heroic imagery, the truth is that Martha's aortic and pulmonary valves are likely to be used for lifesaving surgeries on children with congenital heart conditions, and her brain will be donated to medical science for study and hopefully to save lives in the future.

That is good, I know, and I am really glad of that, but more than anything, I just wish her life had been saved and that she was here with me now. I'm missing her so much, 21 days = 504 hours or 30,240 minutes, during which time every minute has been an hour and every hour a second. Everything is distorted and nonsensical.

I've tried so hard to avoid any yearning and unhealthy thinking as this 'has happened' and I 'must accept it'. But perhaps the initial shock is just wearing off and the tsunami of aftershocks is now hitting the shoreline. Am I safe? Yes, I'm on safe land ... Oh no, I'm not, as there's another tremor and I'm drowning again.

I see Martha's dead body floating on the surface of this sea, her dead face expressionless. It's too late for her, but do I allow my lungs to fill with water or do I float up and fill them with air?

# Tuesday 13th August: Day 24

In every yawn, there's restlessness, in every double-thought there's certainty. I rub my eyes a lot, mostly due to feeling restless, and finding the odd tear on my knuckles is a visual endorsement signifying my loss, despite feeling numb inside.

I am still able to feel a great deal of joy and experience carefree laughter. I don't feel guilty about this as this is who I am. Never have I felt so able to allow my feelings to be whatever they need to be in any given moment. Being utterly vulnerable and neither needing approval from others nor needing the world to understand or love me feels truly liberating.

It's as though I've reached Level 2 of my life. I've earned enough points to move up a level and although there'll be new challenges to face, I've proved I now have enough experience to take on whatever lessons this level requires of me.

I'm in uncharted territory – no map, no signposts, just intuition and common sense. I look around me and it all appears familiar, but my new perspective and intensified awareness of my intuition will navigate me to where I need to go. My itinerary and expectations from Level 1 are redundant and discarded and I am now able to go wherever feels right, so I will allow my instincts to judge situations and will listen accordingly.

While my girl was by my side I was always concerned for her needs, so only having myself to care for does seem peculiar and it'll take a while to get used to this, but there's also a refreshing simplicity about my life now which is gentle and reassuring.

# Wednesday 14th August: Day 25

I feel indifferent today, caffeine, homeopathic pills, diazepam and Martha's funeral plans whizzing around my head. I'm sleeping so well every night, my exhausted eyes close and the darkness engulfs me. I wake every morning as though I haven't slept a wink. Today I remembered the tail-end of a dream from last night which consisted of constant plans and preparations which are keeping my exhausted brain active while my body rests.

We're choosing Martha's burial plot tomorrow, which means I, Anne-Marie Cockburn, age 42, am also choosing my final resting place. This is like no other feeling I can describe: where do I want to end up? Really, I couldn't care less, but as I'm burying my girl, I really *do* care. I need to get this right so that I don't have any regrets about it later. What a decision to have to make.

Helping her decide on what A-levels she'd like to take; helping her work out which university she'd like to go to; helping her settle into her first house or flat: these were decisions I thought I'd need to help her make over the next few years, but where to bury her or choosing my own final resting place were thoughts that never entered my head.

## Wednesday 14th August: Day 25

They've been forced there and no matter how much I deny those thoughts entry, I'm at the point of no return now and I must allow them in. So come on in you unwelcome guests, hold me prisoner and interrogate me until I scream out the answers and give you what you want. I surrender and stick a white flag in her premature grave.

# Thursday 15th August: Day 26

So, here we are, the day I've avoided. I'd rather clean all the loos at Glastonbury than do what we need to do today.

First we drive to the cemetery. I push the doors of the little chapel ajar, it's OK actually, quite sweet really. It's fine – it'll do. Numbers are restricted though as we can only fit in sixty people, but the way I feel at the moment I just want to get it over and done with, so having to restrict the numbers so radically is the least of my worries at this stage.

We wander around the woodland area. It's quite nice, you get to plant a tree and have a tiny plaque indicating your whereabouts, but my uncertainty tells me all I need to know. I prefer the plots to the side of the pathways or at the edge of the woodland – I don't know why, but it just feels right.

Next we drive to the little hall where we'd like to hold her 'after-show party', as I've anointed it. The hall is a little bit out of the way, via a long and winding road, which seems like an appropriate journey to make after burying a teenager. Blind bends to navigate, narrow bridges to get over, fingers crossed that there's no oncoming traffic causing you to retreat and reverse onto the verge, trying to find adequate room that doesn't exist. Travelling on that road is a metaphor for being the parent of a teenager.

We find out the hall isn't available on the day we were hoping for and I don't have a plan B. Making all these decisions is so difficult that when you feel sure you've made the right one, nothing else will do. We stop off for a quick sandwich en route at a pub which I pondered on as a possible suitable alternative venue. There are pigs in the corner and chickens in a coop; it's very Martha, she'd love it, but it'll be partly open to the public and I've got such a personal tribute to my girl planned that it really needs to be completely private.

To the funeral director next; this is the bit I really don't want to do and my demeanour quietly declares this. It feels incredibly outdated and lacking in anything to inspire parents who need to bury their teenager, but I doubt there's a huge demand to warrant catering for our market to the degree I'd like them to.

What are these words my ears are having to hear? I don't want these words to slip into my brain and etch themselves onto my soul, haunting me until my dying day. We're told that she needs to be collected from the hospital mortuary by two men so she can then be taken away to be embalmed. I ask why and am told that it is to deter any decomposition and to reduce the risk of smells emitting from the wicker coffin we've chosen. I feel angry and emotional at the prospect of strangers who don't love her doing this. I don't want this to happen and ask if there is another way we can proceed as this isn't what I want.

I want to collect her from the hospital and take her straight to the cemetery, I don't want her to be embalmed and then moved to a storage unit across town until she gets buried. I want her only to be handled and transported by people who know and love her as I do; I know these people are professionals and will be respectful and honourable, but I just don't want this.

A telephone call is made to the hospital and we're told that Martha can't be embalmed since she will already have started decomposing as it's nearly a month since she died. I take a few deep breaths because, although I'm sitting down, my legs go from beneath me; I'm finding this all too much to cope with.

We're then advised that double-wrapping her may be sufficient to contain as much as possible. My mind is blown, I am spent, I have nothing left to give. I feel as though all the cells in my body are putting up a sign saying 'situation vacant'; they want to depart and find new premises as this one has been condemned.

The cemetery probably won't be able to provide a map of what plots are actually available, they usually just allocate what's there according to religious beliefs, etc. Although they'll try to accommodate based on what you want, they can't promise anything. This surprises me too: can we not choose exactly where my daughter and, in time, I will be laid to rest, based on the plots available?

We're told as we exit the funeral director's that we 'need to collect her as soon as possible', but I'm bewildered as to why since they don't need to embalm her. I leave a voicemail with the chaplain at the hospital asking him to call me back as I want to know if he can give me any advice. I also call the cemetery and speak to a really helpful guy. I explain my dilemma to him and he says he'll do all he can to help me and agrees to meet me tomorrow morning. This sounds hopeful, so that's something at least.

When I get home, I quickly write a list of what the various outcomes were and what needs to be done as my memory is shocking at the moment. I'm barely able to function, even at a basic level.

I lie down, utterly shattered. I now know why I've been avoiding this day. I wish I could have been pre-warned about the discussion in the funeral director's, just a little guidance would have saved me from so much distress. I just really want to do the right thing for my girl – it's the very last thing I will ever do for her, so I want to get it right. I want every little element to contain the essence of her character.

What I've endured over the past few weeks has left me feeling as though I am not even dealing with the remains of my only precious child's body any longer; all this formality, hideous decision making and bizarre discussions. It's like I'm helping to organise an event – a peculiar project – and we've started to get lost in the detail. The 'project' will be delivered and completed in three weeks, that's a given, but we now need to refocus and remind ourselves what we're actually doing here. There is one chance to get this right and I am not going to let this be taken away from me as my beautiful girl was.

# Monday 19th August: Day 30

Today I had just eighty pages of forms to fill in, along with preparation of the various support documentation. You would think I was applying to be the royal nanny, rather than trying to get a little bit of support whilst I convalesce. A family friend came to write it all out for me as I'm barely able to focus, let alone answer questions which would leave someone with a clear mind wondering what the questions really, actually mean.

Could one missing tick cause the system to press the reject button and my entire application to slide down the snake, landing me back at square one? Or will common sense and human decency prevail under the circumstances, meaning that I'd just get a quick phonecall for clarification taking me back up the ladder again?

The A4 envelope is ready and snugly packed full of completed paperwork – everything double-checked, signed and dated. Rather than risk any of the important original backup documents going missing in the post, my family take it directly to the appropriate office to hand it in personally, but are told that they need to send it by recorded delivery. How would I do this without them? How does anybody in my situation get the proper help they need during times like this without being forced to scale walls and dodge the various bureaucratic minefields?

We've reached the planning and action phase – flowers to select, order of service to go over, music and texts to decide upon. It's a peculiar feeling as although I'm desperate to get this next bit over and done with, as every day passes I'm one day closer to it actually happening, so it's a bit like looking forward to something that you know will take you to the depths of despair, and beyond that point who knows where your mind will be, or whether you will have lost your mind altogether.

So it's a heady mixture of foreboding and not wanting your current entire daily schedule to consist of preparation and planning for what's ahead. It's the words 'fear of the unknown', scraped onto your skin with a rusty tattoo needle in big capital letters.

Then what? The cards come down, the flowers wilt and everyone goes home. "Hasn't she got over it yet? It's about time." Will I get avoided in the street as I drag everyone out of their lovely, happy moods, as I become the poster girl for tragedy and remind them of their own mortality? "That's the woman who ..." Now, I can add whatever ending I want to that sentence:

1. The woman who made a difference by raising awareness of the situation Martha left behind, which became a positive legacy for others to learn from.
2. The woman who in time recovered enough to just quietly get on with her life.
3. The woman who never recovered from her daughter's premature death, grew a beard, took in fifty stray cats and is now eating out of wheelie bins.
4. The woman who prevented any other parent from having to endure what she has over the past month.

Right now, I feel as though I am still a woman who wants to help others and to be the best human being I can possibly be, so fingers crossed that when I throw the dice in this snakes and ladders game, I narrowly avoid the snake on box 98 and my little plastic counter taps triumphantly, landing on box 100. That's what I'm aiming for, so fingers crossed, and watch out for snakes.

# Wednesday 21st August: Day 32

A fly buzzes around my living room. I watch curiously as it flies into the window, an invisible glass barrier to the outside world, "Help, get me out of here, I'm stuck in a room with a grieving mother", I hear it buzz. I feel as though my grief is outside the window looking in at me. I know it's there, but I can't smash my way through to it yet as I need to hold myself together for the time being.

Her funeral is two weeks today and there's so much to do. I make some calls and send some emails, then slump exhaustedly onto the sofa. I wrap myself in a soft blanket and snuggle my ears and chin into it. I close my eyes and feel protected as I momentarily pretend none of this is really happening. I take a few deep breaths and with each breath imagine my heart being filled with pure light as a way to remove the heavy dark feeling that's permanently there.

Yesterday I went to the tribute tree as Martha's friends wanted to acknowledge one calendar month. Ten of them had contributed enough money to buy a little plaque inscribed exactly as follows:

For Martha Fernback, The Most Amazing, Effervescent And Funny Girl We Had The Pleasure Of Knowing. 30/10/97 – 20/07/13 Rest In Peace.

They'd laminated loads of post card-sized photos of her and strung them all the way around the tree. They then scattered a box of handmade tissue butterflies into the lake.

What an incredible tribute – leave it to the kids, that's what I say. They are so thoughtful and imaginative. I'd be proud for any one of this group to be my son or daughter.

We hold one minute's silence, then one little friend makes an adorable speech as the rest sob a little and look sad. A van starts to reverse and we hear, "This vehicle is reversing, this vehicle is reversing". My friend says, "That van didn't even know Martha – how dare it make a speech", and we all laugh.

We remain silent and then I hear my voice addressing them all. I say that I am so proud that they are Martha's friends and that she would want them all to be happy. I add that I'd hate for any of their parents to be feeling the agony that I'm feeling right now and that they should have fun, but within the realms of safety – I don't want this experience to hold any of them back in their lives – and ask that they just remember the essence of Martha fondly.

I meet one of the two lifeguards who did CPR on Martha – she has such a beautiful face and I tell her this. I'd heard from a mutual friend that she was suffering from the shock of the whole experience, and we were keen to meet one another. She takes me to the actual spot where Martha unofficially died and we talk quietly and intently as Martha's friends are nearby. I tell her I was glad that someone so caring and lovely was trying to help my girl, but that I'm also sorry she had to experience what she did.

I let her know that Martha was such a happy girl who'd want us to get on with our lives. I'd always said to Martha that she needed to find something she'd love to do with her life, as a life spent doing something you love is a life well spent. I explain that I was privileged to have had fifteen wonderful years with her and that we packed so much adventure into it. This seems to reassure this young woman; I'd hate for this to hold her back in life and continue to haunt her.

So tomorrow I collect Martha's GCSE science results, how peculiar to be doing that. But I'm also intrigued as I know she worked really hard for this exam. I'm proud of my girl regardless of what letter of the alphabet appears on the paperwork to enable others to measure her abilities under exam conditions. Her death has shown me what an impact she'd made in our local community, the entire city and beyond. It's impossible to measure, but evident in every conversation I've had with friends, family and strangers that my girl was like a fifth season, one that would squeeze between summer and autumn – a wisp of beautiful summer sky mixed with the mesmerising, multi-coloured autumn leaves.

If I could speak to her now, what would I say? I'd probably just hold her in my arms, saying absolutely nothing. Happiness in its purest form is held in silence.

She got a B.

# Friday 23rd August: Day 34

It's 2pm and I'm waiting for the reverend from the hospital to arrive with one of his female colleagues. They're helping me to coordinate everything between the hospital mortuary and the funeral director's, for Martha's funeral.

I've just ironed the outfit that I want them to dress Martha in; it's a beautiful cobalt blue tailored playsuit. Wow, what a thing to be doing. She was never bothered about ironing her clothes as she tended to wear leggings or microscopically-skinny jeans which never needed ironing. This is the last time I'll *ever* iron anything for her, but I hate ironing anyway so I don't mind never having to do it again, although it is peculiar and I feel a bit distant from what I'm actually doing.

I've bought two necklaces, there's a left angel wing pendant on one and a right on the other and each is adorned with tiny clear crystals. I'm wearing one and she'll wear the other – it feels like a nice way to link us once she's buried.

My tummy starts to rumble as I'm a little bit anxious about the forthcoming meeting. I know it'll be strange handing over her clothes as it symbolises that we're edging closer to the day of her burial. I run to the loo; what a moment for this inconvenience. I plead that the reverend doesn't turn up any minute now and am grateful that he's a few minutes late due to the nightmare parking restrictions around here.

The meeting is informative and reassuring which is just what I need right now, nothing to worry about and all the most important decisions finally falling into place. My energy levels have totally depleted over the past few days, since the last visit to the funeral director's, which has left me weary and vulnerable. I'm barely even able to walk to the shop on the corner at the moment and I'm wondering how I'm going to get through everything that needs to be done next week. But it'll all work out and so many people have offered to help, so I'll be calling in their offers.

Now that I have the specification of the coffin I need to order, I email it through and follow it up with a phonecall to provide my card details. I then receive an automated phone message from my bank requesting that I confirm that the transaction is legitimate. I try to concentrate on what the automated voice is saying and find it hard to remember, was I supposed to press 1 or 2 if I want to confirm the transaction is OK? Anyway, I get there slowly and manage to approve it. At the end the voice says something along the lines of, "Thank you for confirming your approval of this transaction, but please be aware that this transaction may have been rejected, so please refer to your statement and repeat the transaction if necessary".

On my God, I'm ordering my daughter's coffin, I can't leave it to chance. There's enough money in the bank account, that's not a problem, but the 'computer says "No"' as this transaction is a tad different to my usual spending history. I send through a quick email to the coffin company explaining that I've had a security call from my bank and to call me if they have any trouble on their side of things as we can work something out.

The coffin company then phone me to say that the transaction didn't go through and that they've tried twice – I explain to them that I've had a security call during which I confirmed the transaction is legitimate and that it should all be fine now. If not, then I'll go to the branch on Monday and get them to sort it out. I'm advised that Monday is a bank holiday, but as the coffin only takes four days to make, we'll still be OK if we do it all on Tuesday anyway.

I just want to get this important task done before the weekend and then forget about it. Perhaps Martha didn't like the coffin I chose for her, but that's too bad as she's not here to help me decide. This is all pretty comical. I take a deep sigh and then receive a subsequent email to say that the transaction went through when they tried again. Phew. Honestly, at the other side of all this I feel as though I'd be capable of running NASA or the UN.

So it's Friday night again. The weeks fly by in a blur, five weeks tomorrow Martha died. Five weeks and one day ago, I was driving her back from the beach and she was still alive, we were singing along to the *Lion King* soundtrack and holding hands, leaving our perfect last day together behind us. At that time I had the luxury of planning and expectations for her which I've had to extinguish over the past five weeks in order not to torture myself or prolong the agony.

When I touch the wing pendant on my necklace I stroke the smooth metal back with my thumb and feel my anxiety levels wane a little. As I type I listen to a piece of music on YouTube, Beethoven's Opus 135 (slow), which Martha's friend who plays the cello has put up there. He was away at a music camp in New York when he received the news of her death, so as a tribute, he and three friends all dressed in white and played a string quartet dedicated to her. So incredibly touching, amazing what people do at times like this.

I then listen to the Johnny Cash version of 'You Are My Sunshine', as this was the tune that Martha's cot mobile played to her. Before she was born I searched for weeks to find this tune on a cot mobile as I had a doll that used to play this tune. Every night I'd gently lie baby Martha in her cot, tuck her in and wind up the mobile. A little fabric bee, butterfly, ladybird and snail would rotate as my tiny Martha gazed up in wonder at them from her enormous blue eyes. The words seem enormously poignant to me now:

The other night, dear, as I lay sleeping,
I dream I held you in my arms,
When I awoke, dear, I was mistaken
So I bowed my head and I cried.

You are my sunshine, my only sunshine
You make me happy, when skies are grey
You'll never know dear, how much I love you
Please don't take my sunshine away.

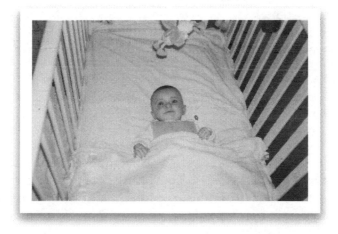

# Monday 26th August: Day 37

My friends took me to a local food festival today. I wasn't sure if I had the energy to walk very far, but I went along anyway although I really just want to be at home all the time at the moment. When the fatigue is permanently there, it's tempting to let it wash over you and give in to it, but I know that it's important to have a change of scenery too.

We borrow a friend's dog and take a back route through meadows and along the river. I've known and explored this city for more than two decades now and it still surprises me when I come across less familiar parts of it and observe it as though I'm a weekend visitor. We pass people walking dogs, joggers, a girl in a canoe and groups punting along the river. The leaves on the trees swish in the breeze and the branches bid us farewell as we pass by.

Apart from styles of clothing, there is very little to indicate which century we're in – everything around us is natural and hiding many secrets. Can passers-by see my secret? Do they look at me and wonder what my story is, as I look at them and wonder what their stories are? Along the way dogs stop to greet the dog we've borrowed and I smile as both people holding the leads smile politely, casting their heads down – this momentary pause linking the two humans together too.

## Monday 26th August: Day 37

We walk on without giving it another thought. Instead, I think about the invisible links my girl made within the world – the momentary pauses she created to link herself to others. If she were alive, would she be walking with us, or would she have made plans to go out with her friends? She'd have loved this walk as she was crazy about animals. Who knows, it's impossible to know, so I stroke the head of the beautiful dog walking alongside me and wish my girl was there instead. "Martha, darling, where are you?" I whisper back to the trees. "Are you here by my side?"

I make it to the food festival and feel OK. As we pass the stalls the steam and aromas waft over me and the sun beats down on us all. We wander around the alleyways of stalls and stop to watch a man demonstrating a whisk which, with very little exertion, creates an impressively firm froth for coffees, and makes a handy baking aid. I walk away feeling certain that it would just end up at the back of a drawer taking up valuable space.

The pain in my heart feels a bit like that. I'm hoping that the valuable space the pain is occupying will be filled up once more with carefree laughter and love of a different type, in time. I look at the crowds of people; there's a tiny toddler in a long vest – he shuffles along swiftly on his little legs, with a dutiful dad in tow to ensure he's out of harm's way. What a journey you have ahead of you, I think, as I watch the father; so many steps to take and things to encounter. I wish you well and hope that your little one is always kept safe.

We get some food and sit in the shade. This is my new normal, I'll have to get used to it as quickly as I got used to the early days of being a new mother. With each step I take on this bizarre journey I move cautiously towards the new chapter. I'm not ready to finish this chapter yet, but at some point I'll bravely turn that page and with a deep sigh I'll just know that it's time.

# Tuesday 27th August: Day 38

My eyes feel blurry this morning as I look out at the clouds, which are blankets of greys and various shades of white. Perhaps summer is over, or perhaps there are still a few unexpected lovely summer days ahead.

I really want this pain in my heart to lift, it's so draining. Last night I read a few online forums for parents who had lost a child and they all say that you never, ever get over it – that's not what I want to hear. I want to get on with my life and find happiness again. I want to love life and to live it with a new-found determination. But I feel as though I'm dragging along an invisible ball and chain with me at the moment.

I don't want this to be it, this is not my legacy, so I can get out there and keep myself busy (distraction method), and remind myself that I may only be halfway through my life – I can choose the road to misery or joy. But I feel as though that choice was taken away from me the day Martha died. Nobody would *choose* the road to misery, but when something so mind-blowingly tragic and final happens – the road to misery chooses you and although you can fight it with every little ounce of strength that you can muster up, it sometimes feels inevitable.

I am normally a positive and happy person, despite having

suffered from bouts of depression years ago, but this isn't depression, I know that for sure – it feels so different. Grieving is totally different. With depression it felt like my mind was pulling me into the darkness and I now realise that back then I wasn't really looking after myself properly, and I didn't understand about 'spotting my triggers' and that positive thinking is key (as is accepting that the past is behind you and that you must press play, rather than rewind).

With grieving it is like you know the rules in order to be happy and you have the tools in which to achieve happiness, but the overwhelming loss you feel renders everything else redundant. Common sense, daily routine, eating well, sleeping well can all still prevail, but grief doesn't seem to listen – it shouts louder.

The online forums also mentioned that people get sick of you not getting over it and in time you turn your friends away from you as they all see you as an atmosphere wrecker. That would be a shame as I've got loads of lovely friends, but what can I do? I can't look at the calendar and see the end date and point out when I'll start to feel better. It's impossible to measure, so I just need to keep living in the minute I'm in, simple as that.

One guy whose son died aged twenty-three mentioned not having any new reference material to talk about beyond that point. At various dinner parties his friends would have new 'material' to talk about in relation to their children, while he was bringing up old stories that they'd heard before, plunging them all into an uncomfortable silence.

So in that case, my new reference material for Martha ran out a few weeks ago now and I may end up being similar to that guy, but what's so wrong with that? I'll always be her mother. I want to talk about her and I want people to join in. I don't want a one-sided conversation for the sake of politeness or to 'just let her get on with it until she's got it out of her system', so they can then talk about real life as they know it. This is real life for me, and Martha will be an eternal flame that remains with me until the end of my days.

This is all so new to me that I'm looking everywhere for the answers, but perhaps I should look online for positive stories of people who have gone on to use their grief in good ways, as that's what I truly want for my own future. Or perhaps I should just believe in my strength and ability to get through this. Martha would want that outcome for me too, so ultimately I do feel that I will recover from this somewhat in time and that the agony will wane. For now I'm bracing myself for her funeral next week and immediately beyond that I'm hoping that I can start to recover and get out into the world to do some good.

# Thursday 29th August: Day 40

Over the last couple of days my energy levels have started to improve, which is great, so I've managed to organise a lot of the arrangements for the party after the funeral. It's such a relief to finally be making some of the more pleasant decisions – choosing decorations for the hall, finalising a little film of Martha, cupcake design for the tea party, what music to play and what photographs to display.

I visualise the hall as I've got it planned: huge colourful paper pompoms hanging at varying heights from the beamed ceiling. Tables of her favourite sweets, pink lemonade served in jam jars to be sipped through red and white paper straws. Dainty sandwiches and cupcakes all lovingly made by people who know me and have a link to Martha. I can see in their faces how much they want to help me to make this an incredible celebration of her life. I know it'll be beautiful, and hopefully people will find some comfort in that.

What do I wear to my daughter's funeral? Part of me couldn't care less, but as soon as I start looking online, I realise that it really does matter to me. I spend hours over the next couple of days looking for a flowery tea dress and late one night I finally find 'the one'. I'm relieved that another decision is made and can be ticked off my list. It's cream with pink roses on; the dress code for the funeral is 'anything that makes you feel happy' so this dress fits the remit perfectly.

The next day an email arrives telling me they've sold out of the dress I wanted and have suggested I select an alternative. I feel really flat – I know it's only a dress, but it's become more than that to me now. It's the last time I'll be a practising mother and I want to show my girl that I haven't given up as I know she'd want me to keep making an effort in my new life. I want to wear my Sunday best and put my lipstick on in order to try to put my best foot forward as my girl is laid to rest.

I'll find something else, but there's not much time now, so maybe I'll just wear something I've already got. I go upstairs and find a vintage dress I bought from a charity shop last year – it's quite sweet. I hang it on the outside of my wardrobe door and say inwardly, "Martha, if you don't like it, then knock it off the wardrobe." The dress falls to the floor. I laugh to myself; coincidence or not, I'm not wearing that dress now.

I receive a phonecall from the funeral directors, who need me to sign a form to secure the burial plot. This phone call tumbles me back into real life from my 'virtual' online shopping dilemma. I dread these calls as I hate going round there, it's so clinical and uninspiring, but then their area of business limits them somewhat and 'safe' good taste must prevail. Why can't it be a warm and inviting place though? Surely there's a mid-way point between traditional and inviting. It's hardly going to be like walking into a boutique hotel, but there's got to be a better way.

I go round and step onto the industrial, bulk-bought carpet and walk past the mini highly polished black granite gravestones which sit on a shagpile rug in the reception area. Change the sign above the door (and remove the gravestones) and you could be standing in a 1970s reception area for a taxi company or the offices of a family-owned solicitor whose best days are behind them.

I'm taken into the meeting room, the same room I nearly passed out in a couple of weeks ago. I don't think about it and just want to get on with signing the form. I'm told it's just a formality, and a finger is pointed to the box they want me to sign. I decide to read the form as so many things have gone wrong to date that I'm not taking any chances. I notice they've ticked the 'single plot' box and without lifting my head up, I cast my eyes over and say, "It's a double plot." They're in a fluster now, "Tell me it's a double plot, please", I say. They're not sure, so I put a squiggle through the single plot box and tick the double plot one to save any doubt as to my wishes. I leave it with them and ask them to check it out and get back to me.

I leave and head into town as I need to buy an extra tie for the undertakers (they're wearing cobalt blue ties to match Martha's outfit). They told us they'd need four, which we ordered online the other day, but a subsequent phonecall advised us that the guy who leads will also need one.

I stand in Marks & Spencer and am surrounded by 'back to school' signs and queuing mums holding armfuls of white t-shirts, socks and underwear. I hear one on her mobile phone making plans and complaining about how little time she has to buy the school uniforms and there's so much to do before 'they go back to school'.

She unconsciously dumps the bundle of clothes on the service desk and without any acknowledgement of the guy serving, carries on with her conversation. She puts her card in at the right moment and taps her pin number in – she could be paying £50 or £500 and would barely flutter an eyelid. She stands side-on and has her elbow on the counter, taking the bag from over her shoulder without so much as a glance at the guy who served her.

As she walks away oblivious to what just happened, I watch in fascination and think how incredibly interesting the whole thing was. I'm fascinated by trivial at the moment, I think perhaps because it is a distraction from all of this serious stuff, although I definitely don't have time for fake in my life now. But I'd like to take trivial on holiday and listen to it spout about how buying PE kits in late August is stressful and tiresome. I'd like to hear how much the kids' feet have grown during the holidays, to the extent that they've outgrown the school shoes that they bought them before holidaying at their family holiday home on an island somewhere owned by an old family friend. I want to hug trivial and say, "Do tell me more, don't stop – I'm listening".

Meanwhile, I'm queuing to buy a tie for one of the guys who will be holding my daughter's coffin. It's fine really, I'm getting used to this strange pocket of time in my life, so my new normal guides me and it's OK, I can do this.

"Next please", says the man behind the counter. I give him eye contact and smile, my phone is tucked away and ignored; being in this room and in the moment is what life is about. Being right here and not always half elsewhere is what will get me through all of this; much as I'd rather remain in my imagination for the rest of my life, I can't allow that to happen. There's a lot in my real life still worth carrying on for.

# Sunday 1st September: Day 43

We're in a new month. This is a surprise to me, but then again, August 2013 will always be the strangest entire month I've ever experienced. My brain is full to bursting with information and 'data' I'd like to download onto a datastick. I'd then put it in a rarely opened drawer and hope that it never sees sunlight again. If only it were that simple, but memories flash through my head without any control, like a toddler who hasn't been taught the meaning of the word 'no' yet.

This past week has actually been relatively enjoyable. I've also totally come off the diazepam and, under the guidance of a homeopath, am now on ignatia, which is the herbal equivalent of Prozac. It's pretty strong stuff. As I let it melt under my tongue, I can feel it permeating my arms and my entire body. It doesn't leave you numb like diazepam, but I can still sense a slight veneer protecting me. I hope it holds me together on Wednesday, I wonder if I've been in too much haste to lose the numbness.

Three more sleeps. I sound like a child asking, "How many sleeps until we go on holiday?" How I wish that is what I was waiting for. One of Martha's friends comes over as I've asked her to put together a little film of Martha to be shown in the hall. She's devoted so many hours to this, as well as caring for the flowers at the tribute tree and helping me to plan all the technical bits I'm no good at.

Other friends join us later to make huge, multicoloured tissue paper pompoms for the hall. By the end of the night the living room looks like the Rio de Janeiro carnival. We talk about Martha, and as we recall little things that she did to make us laugh, the atmosphere is merry and industrious. Martha would love making these pompoms; she'd be right in the middle of it all chatting away.

As my friends look at me, I see my face in theirs. I look into their eyes, and beyond, and know that although I'm doing well, the agony I'm in is obvious. It's as though my friends are peeping over the top of Martha's grave with me and we're all leaning back and looking away from it, back to the colourful pompoms.

I stick the kettle on, as that's what we do. That's what the nurses did for me within minutes of Martha dying – they cupped my hands in theirs as mine were weak and shaky as I lifted the cup to my lips. The same lips that had kissed my girl, the same lips that had advised and helped my girl for nearly sixteen years. The lips that had been full of hope, but were now full of horror. After taking a sip from that cup of tea, I went back in and the same lips kissed my dead daughter's forehead; it was still warm and had until moments ago been full of teenage hope.

A cheeky cuppa as we like to call it – when Martha was little she thought cuppatea was a word. I think we should get the Oxford English Dictionary to add it and the description would say, 'solves everything – malaise, heartache, world peace'.

# Wednesday 4th September: Day 46

I slept for about two and a half hours the night before Martha's funeral; I looked at my phone, which indicated that it was 87% humidity in Oxford. I lay awake thinking about the next day and restlessly tried to will myself to sleep. I was still awake at 3am and then woke again at 5.42am. I got out of bed at 6am on the dot, to the six chimes of the local school chapel tower.

Here we go, I thought. This is it. I came downstairs and sat on the sofa. My breathing has felt restricted the past few days – my throat feels tense and I take a few deep breaths to release the nervous tension in my chest.

I wonder what's ahead today; it's impossible to tell, all I know is that I've put so much into every tiny detail in order to represent Martha authentically and with integrity. I want the essence of her character to show through all the little flourishes I've planned, as though I'm saying, "Sweetheart, this is all for you – do you like what I've done?"

I have a long shower and get ready. I feel restless so I head round to the local patisserie and buy a brick-sized croissant. I need to eat, today of all days. There has to be something in my stomach weighing me down and keeping my feet steadily on the ground. I collect a takeaway coffee and sit out on my terrace as the morning starts to reveal its cards – it's hot already and I'm feeling a mixture of anxiety and relief that it's finally happening. It needs to happen, it can't be put off any further. My girl needs to be laid to rest.

I read over what I'm planning to say today, it's a piece I wrote three days after Martha died, called *Laugh*. It is the right tone – serious enough, but not too gloomy; there are a couple of funny bits in it too, which will give the group a sense of the tone for today along with permission to laugh, as this day is a celebration of her life and an indication of the uniqueness of her character. I mouth the words in a whisper and hope I can project my voice later, as my throat tends to constrict when I'm nervous and I end up sounding a bit croaky.

Public speaking is something I've avoided throughout my life, but I have a sense now that this has all changed since Martha died. I have a message to spread and after what I've experienced over the past six and a half weeks, I feel I'm the right person to talk about it.

A friend comes to collect me and we head to the cemetery, which has a small chapel in the middle where the service will be held at 11am. J.R.R. Tolkien is also buried in this cemetery and the poet Elizabeth Jennings – Martha would probably have liked this … maybe she wouldn't, but it's interesting all the same. I read the entry on Wikipedia about the cemetery and learn that 15,000 people are buried there – 15,001 now, I think. A new special girl is coming to join you.

I keep taking the odd deep breath to clear my head and mentally prepare myself for what I need to do today. I don't want to 'lose it' too early on and end up feeling sad that I wasn't able to say what I needed to.

The plot I wanted is ready. I walk up to it and stare in – it's very neatly done, there's a huge mound of dirt to the left of it, covered by a blanket of green astroturf. I set a little 1950s table down and put a dusty old metal gramophone speaker on it along with a miniature bicycle. I'm so happy I got this plot as we weren't sure if the tree roots would affect it or not. I look at the 'Granddad' wreath on the plot next to ours and feel comforted by that. This feels right and I'm relieved to not be freaked out by the sight of it all.

We go into the chapel and work out where to fit the two cellists and violinist. My daughter's friend is an incredibly talented fifteen-year-old cellist who will be playing along with his parents, both of whom are astoundingly gifted musicians. Martha had spent time at their home and spoke very fondly about how lovely they were to her, so this seems like a wonderfully fitting accolade today.

We move some seats around and try to visualise who should sit where and how it will all work. People start to arrive and I ask them to wait outside as I want them all to be there for when Martha arrives, to welcome her. I feel tense and irritable as the inevitable is looming. I'm concerned that not everyone will fit in as the chapel is tiny and the pews are very small. I hope nobody uninvited turns up and have shared my concern with the cemetery manager that the press will – I've made it clear that this is private and 'by invitation only', so the cemetery staff are on high alert.

My friends and I sit in one row to work out the spacing and see how many of us can fit on one of the smaller pews – it's fine, we think, people will just have to budge up. It may be a little bit uncomfortable, but the service isn't long anyway – 30 minutes at the most.

The funeral director tells me that 'she's arrived' a little bit early and that they've parked at the main gates. I feel my nerves jar at this news; I take a deep breath in and hold it to calm myself. I walk outside into the sunlight and am greeted by a circle of people who represent all the years of my life. My own living Wikipedia, I step from person to person, hugging each in turn; my mouth moves – but I don't know what I'm saying to them.

I wave at faces further away and give them a meek smile. I stand alone as I wait for my girl to arrive – it was always just her and me, the two of us, so it seems fitting that I stand alone, waiting for her to join me as I always have. The funeral director indicates that they're going to start slowly driving up the driveway and that he's heading over to walk in front of the vehicle.

We wait and wait. I twist my arms and clamp my fingers and palms together as though I'm holding her hand in mine as a way to try to comfort myself in this moment. After what seems like half an hour, I see a beautiful white classic VW camper van hearse glisten ahead of me. Here we go, I say to myself.

I am relieved by how beautiful it looks – I'm not spooked by this either. My girl is here and it all looks so magical. We spent the day before she died on the beach – that idyllic day that I will always be eternally grateful for – so the campervan is entirely fitting. I always said that I would take her away in a campervan one day, but I couldn't ever have imagined that it would be like this.

I hear the ticking rhythm of the well-timed old engine – it's as though it's comforting me and saying, "All is well dear – no need to worry yourself", like an old granddad would. They park in front of the little chapel and open the back door, lifting it up towards the roof. The wicker coffin is utterly beguiling, blanketed by an array of wild meadow grasses, blackberries, daisies, tiny pink roses, cornflowers and moss and dotted with white paper butterflies. I feel so joyful, it feels as though an enormous black ball of tension has left my chest and been cast away in the warm breeze. For the first time since Martha died I feel that she is with me in spirit. I now realise I've felt buried alive for the past six and a half weeks.

I catch glimpses of cobalt blue from the cornflowers, which match the ties of the undertakers, which match in my mind with the playsuit that Martha's wearing – it all works so well. We're told we need to wait before taking her into the chapel as we're a little bit ahead of schedule. I feel restless as I want this next bit to be over with. I don't feel distressed by the sight of the coffin, which is reassuring. I've visualised it for so long, as though I've been in training for a marathon and that training has finally paid off.

We're given the signal to proceed so they gently slide her coffin out and delicately lift her shoulder high. As they adjust their position and prepare to walk her in, the flowers gently wiggle around. I proudly walk behind her as though she's at her first day of primary school all over again – this is my girl, isn't she adorable? They set her down on two wooden plinths in the aisle and we all take our places as the cello music fills up the tiny chapel and lingers in the air outside.

OK now, nearly there, I think. I look at the rope handles of the coffin and layers of woven wicker; I can see tiny specks of light – "Hello my darling girl – nice to have you beside me again." The service starts. It's a humanist service; humanism is based on being a loving human being and this is how I brought my girl up.

I've decided to speak after the official introduction and I find myself floating up the small step to the lectern – I'm OK actually. I'm a little bit emotional, rather than nervous. I find my voice – I hear my words and feel composed and poised. My head is clear, each paragraph flows and I feel as though I'm nourished by every word.

I deliver the first funny line and the room fills with laughter – I wish laughter were a currency and for every laugh you give someone, they pay back with one. My girl made so many people laugh, it was definitely her main currency and way of communicating.

I deliver the second funny line and everyone laughs again; this feels gentle and lovely. I didn't read this piece for the laughs, but in the moment I'm so glad that we can all sit in a room alongside my girl's coffin and feel joy rather than utter despair. I sit down and watch my friend take her place at the lectern to read an excerpt from Martha's favourite book, *Kensuke's Kingdom* by Michael Morpurgo:

Washed up on an island in the Pacific, Michael struggles to
survive on his own. With no food and no water, he curls up
to die. When he wakes, there is a plate beside him of fish,
of fruit, and a bowl of fresh water. He is not alone . . .

Another friend then takes her place at the lectern and reads the
following:

"The fluttering of a butterfly's wing can affect climate changes on
the other side of the planet." – Paul Erlich


**'After a while' by Veronica A. Shoffstall**

After a while you learn
the subtle difference between
holding a hand and chaining a soul
and you learn
that love doesn't mean leaning
and company doesn't always mean security.
And you begin to learn
that kisses aren't contracts
and presents aren't promises
and you begin to accept your defeats
with your head up and your eyes ahead
with the grace of woman, not the grief of a child
and you learn
to build all your roads on today
because tomorrow's ground is
too uncertain for plans
and futures have a way of falling down
in mid-flight.
After a while you learn
that even sunshine burns
if you get too much
so you plant your own garden

and decorate your own soul
instead of waiting for someone
to bring you flowers.
And you learn that you really can endure
you really are strong
you really do have worth
and you learn
and you learn
with every goodbye, you learn...

We have a moment to reflect whilst Bach's Goldberg Variations is played. I hear people sobbing behind me. Martha's little friend playing the cello looks at me and smiles – I smile back at him, it's a truly magical piece of music. I look at her coffin again: "What do you think Martha, isn't it beautiful?" They're here for you, they truly love you – you can hear this in every single note of music.

I get up again to read a poem I found within three days of her death. It was on my laptop, but I have no recollection of downloading it or ever reading it prior to that day. It's called 'Magic':

Imagine for a second that the world you live in is magic.
Not your hocus-pocus, wave-your-wand-magic,
but magic like the coffee tables you sit at beat
with the hearts of the trees they were made from.
That the coffee and beer in your mouths
is feeding you life straight off the tongues
of the plants they were made from.
That every heart beating in this room
is beating in time to every heart in this room
and this poem.

Some of you will go home with some of you tonight
and some of you will go home to empty rooms

that some of you will wish you had gone home to:
go home to them.

Your empty rooms and the rooms you fill
always have at least one poem in them.
There is a poem in the pretty girl eyes in the front row
and there is a poem in the old man's cigarette on the porch
and there is a poem in the coffee girl's hands.
There is a poem in your hands, if you'll look for it

Imagine for a second that the world you live in is magic,
    because it is.
Because when you go home to your empty rooms
or to the rooms you fill you each take some of each of you
    with you,
if you want it.

If you want it,
you can take some of the pretty girl's poem
and you can take some of the old man's poem
and you can take some of the coffee girl's poem
and you can take some of mine.

Tonight, when I go home, my room will be empty,
and I will fill it with your poems.
I will fill it with the life the beer and coffee have fed you.
I will fill it with the heartbeats the tables you sit at
have beat against your hands.
I will fill it with the kisses that some of you will give to
    some of you
and I will fill it with the kisses that some of you
will wish you had been kissed with.
There is a poem shaking the air your ears are listening to.
Listen to it. Go home and look into eyes you've never
    looked into.
Hold a hand you've never held.

Touch flesh you've never been touched by.
Open your mouths and fill yourselves up
with every poem in every person you encounter tonight.
I'll do the same.
The world you live in?
It's magic.

Gabriel Gadfly (© Gabriel Gadfly http://gabrielgadfly.com)

As they start to lift Martha's coffin up, I place the palm of my hand gently on the side of it. They lift her shoulder high again and we walk her the short distance to her grave. As I walk out of the chapel I smile at the beautiful sea of faces looking at me. I'm writing this piece only one day later, but I have no recollection of my walk from the chapel to the grave, but I do know that I felt peaceful. I remember them setting her coffin down on two wooden supports over the grave as I stood by one end. I thank her for the wonderful fifteen years we had together and say that I feel privileged to have had that.

I feel calm as she is lowered into 'our' grave; a white butterfly flies in and lands on her coffin to join her on her final journey, as though patting her gently. It then flies back up and flutters around up into the trees and sky. The music in the background is the old Disney song 'When You Wish Upon a Star' which Martha had starred as a favourite on her online music account; the old man's voice gently warbles and echoes out of the gramophone speaker into our ears and through the soles of our feet to Martha's new neighbours beneath the ground.

I pick up Martha's plastic popcorn container, which I've filled with silver stars. I take a handful and cast them into the grave; I watch them arch up and it's as though someone momentarily presses pause. In slow motion the stars cascade down catching twinkling rays of sunshine as they fall – I'm mesmerised by how magical it looks. I hand the container around and each person in turn comes along to scatter stars in. People then come up to hug me as they leave her grave; these hugs are full of hope for my happy future and love for my girl, who's lying behind them.

I stand on the edge of the plot and peer in at her coffin, which is covered with stars. The slim coffin doesn't fill the plot fully and I see the soil around her glistening with stars too, filling the void. As in her life, although she was tiny and didn't physically take up very much of the space around her, her character filled every room to bursting point. I feel all the tension from the past six and a half weeks leaving me and a calming peace descends.

We make our way to the village hall for Martha's party. I'm greeted by a friend's whippet dog that I first knew as a puppy. He barks affectionately as I pat him; Martha worshipped this dog. We'd always jump at the chance of a doggy sleepover session – he'd head up to Martha's room in the middle of the night and scratch her door until she woke up and let him in to snuggle up with her. I'd find them in the morning curled up together like siblings, skinny little legs poking out everywhere from the crumpled duvet.

Over the years we toyed with the idea of getting a dog, but we'd always conclude with the words, "Yes, but it wouldn't be Zephyr", and we'd leave it at that. Here is her dog back to say hello to me; I wonder if he can see her as I've heard that dogs have a sixth sense like that.

Zephyr leads me into the hall and the tissue pompoms dangle above our heads like orb-shaped rainbows. People are dotted around in little groups, the heat is immense and as everyone greets me I feel their damp cheeks against mine. I stop to chat and work my way around as many people as I can.

The quiet reflection room we set up is filled with photos and Martha memorabilia – her white Converse All Star Hi-Tops, her first babygro, the ankle tag from when she was born. A long L-shaped table holds hundreds of condolence notes and cards which have been posted to me or left at the tribute tree.

The photos from our last perfect day on the beach are set out on three A2-sized foam boards in chronological order, including the very last ever photograph of Martha. Hundreds of photos have been hung on string, secured with tiny wooden clothes pegs. A condolence book is set up on a table for people to express anything they feel moved to write in the moment.

We have twenty-four seconds of Martha playing 'L'Après–Midi' by Yann Tiersen, which will be projected onto a screen, and my friend is poised to play from the twenty-four second point onwards. I tell everyone what's about to happen and they watch intently. We look to the stage at the screen and there is my girl alive and well, dreamily playing on the piano, you can hear my friends and me chatting and joking around her. It works beautifully from the screen to my friend who carries it on – it's stunningly poignant.

We then show a brief film that her friend and I have put together, which shows video clips, photos from her life, including cute excerpts which make us all laugh, and footage of the tribute tree which makes us all remember what we're here for. I feel the emotion in the room, but I also feel a mixture of pride knowing how much I did for her over the past fifteen years and the colourful life that I managed to provide.

Within a couple of hours people start to leave and we're eventually left with a group of close friends who help to clear everything up. It's orderly and civilised; I wander around not doing anything particularly useful, apart from indicating what needs to go where. A friend mops the kitchen floor and we head to the door with the black bin bags and leftovers.

Our group stands outside and the hall is locked up. As it's only 4.30pm I suggest we go to sit by the river at the nearby meadow, as this is a spot I took Martha regularly to swim. It's boiling hot as we arrive and some friends head off home to get changed then come back. I didn't feel it was appropriate to serve alcohol at Martha's funeral, but I fancy a glass of something to celebrate now that everything is over. I'm fatigued, but happy – I really can't believe how well it all went and how joyful the whole thing was.

I make a toast to the new chapter I have just begun and normal floats gently back to surface. "Hello," I say, "welcome back old friend, good to see you again".

# Thursday 5th September: Day 47

I wake up early, as at 5.45am I receive a text from a friend who is travelling back to London to get to work – he had come up for the funeral. He is watching the beautiful sunrise, which makes him think of Martha. This makes me smile and I'm feeling good at the start of this new day beyond 'the day'.

I want to write immediately and document yesterday in as much detail as possible while I'm feeling refreshed and my head is clear. I write for three and a half hours and 2,605 words later, I've written up until the moment I leave the cemetery. I want to go to the grave this morning, so I leave writing about the party until later today when I have a bit more time.

I decide to stop taking the homeopathic medication now as I want whatever emotion arises to be allowed to surface, so I can deal with it and get on with my life.

I haven't cycled since before Martha died; she'd used my bike on her last day, so as I cycle up to the cemetery I think of her little body sitting on this saddle and her little legs peddling to kayaking. It's a hot day again and I'm feeling good as my strength is returning. Yesterday was a particularly dreaded milestone that was a lot more enjoyable than I could ever have hoped for.

## Thursday 5th September: Day 47

I cycle through the metal gates at the main entrance to the cemetery and visualise the campervan sitting to the right the day before, containing my precious Martha. I see her flowers along my line of vision and I swing my leg over and coast for a few meters, jumping off when I near the tree next to her plot. I lean my bike against the tree and look over the line of graves that Martha's at the end of.

I look at the temporary name plate fixed on a small wooden stake; I lift it out of the soil and examine the words. I take a photo and see my own face reflecting back at me. I look tired and thin. I've brought a copy of 'Style' magazine for her, which is a homage to our Sunday morning routine as we'd always get 'Style' magazine and go out for coffee. We'd share the odd fashion page and talk about that week's entries on the Mrs Mills page.

Every Sunday since Martha died my friends and I have maintained this tradition. They've lovingly taken me out for coffee or turned up with takeaway coffees and the newspaper under their arm. It's a comforting and wholesome ritual for me now.

Friends have been to the grave to water her flowers which are still looking bright and healthy. I stand by the grave and feel as though my girl is with me, it feels nice to be able to visit her place of rest. I know she's not really 'there' as her spirit was so much more than just her body, but I am surprised by how much comfort being here provides me.

I sit on a nearby bench and look across the array of gravestones and flowers. I see a squirrel scurrying from right to left with a huge piece of greenery in its mouth. It stops momentarily to nibble away and then runs on again before making a left-hand turn and running in my direction. It rolls on its back and then skids along on its stomach. Passing a plant pot it jumps up onto it but its back legs slip and fall over the edge; it tries to jump up again, only to fall backwards onto the grass. I laugh and can't take my eyes off it as it's such a hilarious little character.

I get back on my bike and cycle through the gate. This is the first time I've visited my girl here – there'll be lots of 'firsts' for me from this point onwards, but now that the funeral pressure is off my shoulders I'm feeling happy again.

I'm meeting a friend for breakfast and as I cycle towards the sun the angel wing necklace clinks and I think of the other wing, which Martha is wearing. My friend and I talk about yesterday in detail; he thought it was truly incredible too. He admits that he'd been dreading it, but that he'd felt it was joyful and uplifting.

He was a big fan of my daughter. The two of them would sit in a local café and play backgammon (he'd always lose) and she'd tease him, calling him Mr Taramasalata due to his Greek heritage. He tells me he'll always light a candle for Martha throughout his life and I'm touched at what a lovely gesture it is.

I head home and finish writing up my account of yesterday. The party at the hall piece doesn't seem to flow as well as the piece at the cemetery. I'm tired and it's hard to recollect every single relevant moment as there is so much to recall. It seems like a bit of a haze now, but I do my best and end up writing a total of 3,376 words to represent that day.

I've arranged for a child bereavement counsellor to meet me at my home at 4.30pm. I'm not sure if I need it, but felt that it was a sensible thing to organise. I saw her once before, a couple of weeks after Martha died. She has a very gentle approach and I like her observations. She usually works with parents of terminally ill children at a local hospice, so my case is slightly different from usual, but she's perfect for my needs and I feel at ease in her company. She said that another mother two years after her child's death described grieving as 'a sentence that you're at the mercy of'.

## Thursday 5th September: Day 47

After this I put the wheelie bins out for tomorrow as I've missed them for about the last six weeks. A friend and I jokily dance around the street with the bins and lift the lids as though they're mouths – people pass giving us strange looks which is understandable, but they don't know the journey we've taken to this point over the past month and a half. They'd dance with us if they knew.

I've now written a total of 4,280 words today and I'm completely exhausted and ravenously hungry. Day one of the new chapter was fulfilling and hopeful.

# Sunday 8th September 2013: Day 50

It's Sunday morning, so here we go. I try to stay in bed beyond 6am, but keep waking up ridiculously early. I lie in bed reading a book bought for me. It's called *Wave: A Memoir of Life After the Tsunami* and is about a woman who lost her husband, two boys and her parents in the Boxing Day tsunami. As I read it and hear her description of how angry and bitter she felt, I'm surprised I feel so different to that. She also expresses a constant desire to kill herself, which I definitely don't have.

Some friends and I went out for dinner last night; the atmosphere was busy but relaxed. I felt OK. It was Saturday night and good to be at the other side of everything. The food was delicious and the conversation was nice. I was mindful not to hog the conversation with anecdotes about Martha, but it's all I want to do if I'm honest. I want to keep her alive, to save me from becoming a living dead person.

It's like studying for sixteen and a half years and becoming an expert in your field only for the industry to say that they don't need you now. So what do you do with all that expertise? What do you talk about? What do you do now? There is no plan B, but you're forced to consider other options. Your head is full of advice and specialist knowledge, but you're now re-referencing your own future and you're currently faced with a mire to wade through.

As we neared the end of the evening I felt twitchy and desperate to get home. A girl was wearing a pair of the same white Converse All Star Hi-Tops as Martha was wearing when she died and I was sitting at exactly the same table as I was the last time I was there with her. There are so many constant reminders that I must learn to cope with, rather than allow myself to be upset by.

I feel emotional today as I know 'this is it now'. Things have gone quiet and people have said, "You know where we are if you need us", but to me it's clear I'm really on my own now and that it'll take *me* to keep me together. My home is full of boxes and bags brought back from the funeral party. I can't face organising them yet, but the disarray around me is also cluttering my head, so I must sort through them soon.

I get a takeaway coffee and buy the *Sunday Times*. A friend and I get the bus up to the cemetery. We flick through 'Style' magazine and ask Martha what she likes. We leave it for her and look around, noticing that there are little groups of people dotted about – a club I'm a new member of. I wonder if I'll get to know the families of Martha's new neighbours – what a strange thought, but it's valid all the same. It's cold today and I'm feeling unsettled, so we don't stay for long.

I've planned to go with a friend to stay with her parents in Derbyshire. We pack enough for two days and head off. I'm emotional as this marks the start of new things and although it's important for me to remain motivated, it hurts all the same to be doing this without her. On the floor of the bus there's a cardboard lid from a box of family size tissues – I don't need these now I think, I only need single packs. Can a family consist of one person? Am I my family now?

At the railway station, I ask if I'm able to use my Family Railcard, but they advise that at least one child needs to travel with us (she is with us, I think to myself, but not in the physical way you're meaning). It's another first for me. Martha and I loved travelling by train and I bought an annual Family Railcard every year as it saved us a fortune, but I can't get this discount now without her. The other Railcard options are for 16–25 year olds, or senior citizens. I don't fit into any of these categories; I'm out on my own, I can't be categorised and I need to find comfort in that, rather than the sorrow and abandonment I'm currently feeling.

I walk out onto the platform for the first time without her after all these years. This platform has shipped us off on many a trip, she and I, full of anticipation and adventure. It takes my breath away and I gulp in air to stop myself from sobbing. Today I'm with a dear friend, who allows each moment I need and gently listens to my ramblings. She quietly observes my tears but I worry I'll eventually drive her away.

We cross the bridge and wait on the platform as the train approaches – little does it know that it's taking me on my very first journey in my new state. A very special and painful journey. I look at the train square-on and take my first big step up into the carriage. "Hello", I say to my new self, which is shy and wary, as am I. My new self says a confident hello back. "I've been waiting for you, take a seat. We've got a lot to organise."

## Monday 9th September: Day 51

I travelled into Sheffield by tram today; I felt as though I could have been in Italy or heading to an airport on the shuttle. It was nice to be away from everything familiar. I look at the blur of unfamiliarity speeding past me as we trundle along. My girl was the perfect travel companion; we had travelling down to a fine art from years of exploring the world.

She knew I'd get a bit stressed heading to the airport. I always preferred to get there early, check in and then relax with extra time on our hands, rather than leave anything to the last minute. She'd take in my curt responses without reacting as she knew what I needed during those moments.

As we wander around the city centre, I catch reminders everywhere. It's good to be here, I tell myself, good to get away. I carry her in my heart, the pain is in my heart. In every glimpse there is something and I feel as though I'm trying to erase my memories as it's torture. But I don't want to erase her, I worked too hard for sixteen and a half years and made Martha a huge priority in my life. It's not something you can write off overnight, or ever, for that matter.

We walk to Ecclesall Road as a friend has recommended we head there to potter around the shops and find a café for lunch. It's about twenty minutes of walking, during which we observe the locals going about their lives and look at the different styles of houses and shops. It's good to be away from familiar territory, I tell myself again.

For lunch we find a great restaurant, which has an impressive menu. We're all tired and famished and eager to eat. If she was here, what would she order? I look over the options and wonder. She never really ate much, my little twig, as I nicknamed her. When she died she was about 6 and a half stone and 5 foot 5 inches tall. I never, ever saw her overeat throughout her entire life – she'd get full on half an ice-cream and would throw the other half in the bin. At times this waste annoyed me, but she knew her limits and this was just how she was.

My phone rings at the end of lunch, it's my doctor doing a welfare check on me. I excuse myself from the table and take my phone to a chair in a quiet corner. The tears start to fall immediately. She asks how the funeral went and I tell her how lovely it was. I tell her I'm in a lot of pain and that I know there aren't any answers and that is the problem. What is there to say? What can anyone say to me to take the agony away?

I feel as though my heart is constrained and my throat is constricting, I need to get outside. I tell my doctor I need to get off the phone, she tells me she'll call again in a couple of weeks. I then tell my friends that I need to get out of here straightaway. I feel panicky and emotional. I open the door and feel the cool air hitting my face, which gives immediate relief. I felt as though I was having a heart attack in there.

As we slowly walk back to the city centre, a little girl crosses our path; her dad is holding her hand and carrying her book bag. She's wearing Mary Jane shoes and jumping up and down at the crossing, stopping momentarily to go up on her toes as they wait for the lights to change. I hear her shoes tapping the road behind us as they make their way across. I don't look back.

I'm in Sheffield, my little girl is lying in her grave in Oxford and her brain is at a specialist London hospital for further tests to be carried out. This is all too much for me. How am I supposed to do this? Truly, how? It's incomprehensible. I just don't know what I'm expected to do with all this stuff in my head, memories and numerous shocks from the past few weeks. Demons and madness are flooding my veins and penetrating my heart – they're running amok and I'm fighting them every step of the way, but they're gaining strength as I tire. The white flag is there in the corner taunting me – go on, wave me, give up. No, I say, I can't.

The demons press my heart, one pushing from the left and one from the right. I put my hand to my chest and take a slow, deep breath. Give me what Martha took then I can join her – half a gram of white powder and I'd die deliriously happy too, as high as a kite and full of love and rainbows. What would be the point of that though? I've got work to do, people to help. I have a vocation and that is why I'm here going through this agony, so others can learn from this experience.

Back on the tram we pass rows of houses and I see a woman holding a baby in her arms, looking out of an upstairs window – that was me all those years ago. Just Martha and me. Look at the world little one, isn't it wonderful? It is, I think, even in my present state. It is, so lead me back to peace and happiness and let me feel carefree once again.

Tonight the reality is sinking in as I realise I'm not going to wake up from this. I look out of the car window as we're driving along the motorway and I feel as though dying in a car crash would be less painful than what I'm feeling right now. Give me half a gram of the same stuff that killed Martha as there is no life in what

I'm experiencing. This isn't living, it's hell and the suffering I'm enduring is unimaginable. How do I get through this?

Once again my heart feels as though someone is squashing it between their hands in a vice-like grip and I'm writhing in pain – nobody is hearing my cries for help. I'm shouting from inside a huge glass cloche that's covering me. Who is listening to me? Who can help me? Who can take this pain away? "Nobody", comes the whispered answer. "Only you can get yourself through this", it says.

One consolation I'm desperately feeding myself through all this pain is that every time I endure a moment of agony, it will take me one step through my recovery and out the other side. Please let that be the truth.

How do I do this? Can I do this, more to the point. Am I up for this? Who could possibly be up for this experience? Where do I go from here? New 'normal' is joyless, like an endurance test I didn't sign up for. I don't want this, no matter what you tell me. Beyond this is something I haven't planned for and am not prepared for on any level. My future history was mapped out for me to a degree but I'm now looking into a desolate wasteland. It's dark and gloomy and I'm alone, and a shadow of my former self.

Tell me the answers, show me the way, take my hand and tell me what to do. I am a dead leaf in the wind, floating around, reacting to the elements and settling momentarily, shaking around a little and then being swept back up into the sky to land again upon each new day. Some days are gentle and some are bumpy; I'm at the mercy of the elements. We all are, to a degree. Mother nature is in charge, so I'll let her mother me and snuggle lovingly into her bosom. There, there, she whispers. She kisses my forehead and I fall gently to sleep.

# Thursday 12th September: Day 54

I've started to live my life in segments. I break a little piece off and digest it; today's segment is entitled 'starting to clear my home'. I look at her coat hanging by the kitchen door, put my hand in the pocket and find some sweets – they're luminous yellow tiny balls called 'millions'. We had a pick 'n' mix table at her funeral party and had all her favourite sweets laid out along with little paper bags for everyone to select what they wanted. There were Flying Saucers, heart-shaped jelly sweets, Smarties and Drumstick lollipops as well as Tunnock's Teacakes and Jammie Dodger biscuits.

I inefficiently move piles of framed photos from the kitchen table to the living room; I restlessly place them around the room without any consideration to order or sense.

Yesterday was a good day, I was back at home and felt safe again. My chest is more at ease, despite the permanent pain in my heart. I went into town with a couple of friends. St Giles Fair was being cleared up. This is a two-day long fair which takes over the wide road of St Giles in the heart of Oxford. My little Martha set up and ran the St Giles Fair Facebook page for about the past four years. She was like that, she did it of her own accord and would start a countdown – '5 days to go people … can't wait'. There were over a thousand followers. She'd go every year after school

on the afternoon of the first day. One year her friends were being
funny with her, so she went by herself – I loved the fact that she
wouldn't let this deter her from enjoying herself – and she had a
great time regardless.

The good thing about being an only child is that you can
entertain yourself quite happily, but Martha also thrived in a
family environment and loved going to have dinner with friends
in their family homes. She'd always eat more when sitting
around the table with other children, rather than when it was
just the two of us eating at home.

Over the past few days various strange thoughts have passed
through my head such as should I have another baby? Would
this child be held back by what's happened to Martha; would I
worry myself sick and make this child's life hell? I was 26 when I
became a mother; you need so much energy to bring up a child,
so this was beneficial. I was so looking forward to going out as
mother and daughter for dinners and to share a glass of wine or
two as grown ups.

Is forty-two too old and do I have the energy to start again? I
know you can't replace one human being with another, but I
can't help these feelings as being a mother is such a natural thing
for me. Admittedly, I was more prepared to be a grandmother
at some point in the next fifteen years, than a mother again.
I've got a box of Martha's baby things which I was planning on
passing to her for her own babies. Where do I put them now?
I'm not even in a relationship, so it's not as though it's a realistic
proposition and I know that I'm in no fit mental state to make
any serious decisions right now.

A friend visits with her six-month-old baby girl – I gather her
in my arms and smell her little fluffy head and rock her gently.
Could I do this again? I wonder to myself. I don't really think
I could. The pain makes me want to, but grieving does strange

things to you. It makes you want to fill that pain and the gap Martha represented, but I know it doesn't work like that in practice.

I know it's important to work through any issues you have before making life-changing decisions. I think the most sensible solution for me is to be a wonderful and devoted aunt or godmother, rather than a mother who would be nearing sixty years old before my child would reach nearly sixteen years old again. That doesn't sound right for me, so I'll leave it in the lap of the gods, try to welcome each moment (or segment) and allow it to be whatever it needs to be.

# Friday 13th September: Day 55

I looked up what half a gram of powder looks like on Google yesterday. Such a tiny amount of powder wiped out a beautiful human life. If she had taken a tiny bit less, would she be here right now or was her number up regardless?

It's drizzly outside, the sky is grey and the trees are completely still. It looks like a photograph; nothing is moving, but I can hear the traffic to indicate signs of life. I hear the bin lorry and realise I've forgotten to put the green wheelie bin out yet again. How can it be Friday again already? Eight weeks to the day tomorrow ... I've lived ten lifetimes in the past eight weeks. The summer is but a blur to me; I have no recollection or memories of what my girl and I did together this summer apart from the horror story that unfolded. One to forget, but there's no chance of that happening.

I imagine myself as an elderly woman and wonder what will be going through my head then. Will I have kept Martha alive in my memory; will she always be there or will that be too much of a burden? I'm sure I'll always think about how old she would be had she still been alive. I'm sure I'll think of her when I see her friends settling down and embarking on their careers and marriages and I'll look up and wonder. The luxury of choice, I think. My choices aren't entirely limited, but what I would really choose isn't within the realms of possibility.

Tonight my parents are taking me out to dinner. This will be our first family dinner without Martha. Another first, but they all have to happen. The word Christmas pops into my head and I promptly dismiss it. It rattles my brain and my head spins. Shops full of sparkly stuff and music on repeat driving the staff mad. We'll all be going mad, but for different reasons. "Oh I wish it could be Christmas every day ..." hmmm ... I wish it could be 19th July 2013 and I was having an important conversation with Martha about drugs and she really understood the dangers rather than the allure, and her death was avoided. I wish.

I speak to my mum who tells me she's ill. Poor thing, she's seen me almost die of shock over the past two months and is grieving over the loss of her first grandchild, her immune system must be shot. I'm relieved that we're cancelling the first Martha-free family dinner, but it's only putting off the inevitable. Like the funeral, it has to happen sometime.

I receive an email and see the words 'sorry for the loss of your child' within the text. Loss? I think. She's not lost – I almost wish she were. But she's not coming back. I then think of Madeleine McCann's family and wonder how it must be when there's a glimmer of hope that your child is still somewhere on this planet. You wouldn't stop searching, you'd never stop hoping and believing; as long as there's a possibility that her child's heart still beats, a mother can feel it inside her own.

# Saturday 14th September: Day 56

I finished reading *Wave: A Memoir of Life After the Tsunami*. It was so important to me that there would be a happy ending by the final page and that all was well but I didn't impulsively skip to the final page to have a peek. I wish I could do this with my own life – put me in a coma for three years and then wake me up – but I know I'd just have to contend with it then, so I need to 'read and write' every page of my own current life in order to reach the final page, and that is why I studiously read every page of this book.

It wasn't clear whether it was a happy ending or not – that woman went through hell, so what do I know? She didn't go into as much detail as I have, but then again, she lost five members of her immediate family. I did recognise a common thread in places and that was reassuring. When she found her husband's eyelash on the pillowcase I fully understood how such a usually insignificant thing became so powerful and meaningful; a symbol of that person's existence alongside yours.

I gave Martha's watch to a dear friend of hers. He showed me the hole she used to wear it on as her wrist was so tiny in comparison to his; he pointed to it and I could see it was slightly worn with a faint line going across the strap. A sign of her life in the present day feels comforting.

I wanted the ending of the book to have an 'in your face', spoon-fed happy ending, but I'll just need to create my own. We all react differently to situations and to trauma, so you can't just buy a *Grieving for Dummies* guide and compartmentalise it like that ('turn to Chapter 5 for top tips and exercises on what to do with that A5 brown envelope of your child's hair perched on your mantelpiece'). It's all so complex and incredibly personal.

I phoned Vodafone today to discuss Martha's mobile phone contract, which I'm still paying for and doesn't expire until March 2014. After being held in a queue for a few minutes a girl came on the phone laughing. I paused and waited for her to speak. With laughter in her voice she started reading her script. I was incensed; I asked her if she was ready to speak to me as I needed someone mature who could help me sort out something very serious.

My tone hit her like a hammer as she realised that she'd just pulled the short straw. I don't want to wear Martha's death like a badge, but at certain moments you just can't help it. Her voice started to shake and she said "Bless her soul" and asked me how I was. I said "I'm fine, but just need to get this sorted by someone who is capable of providing the appropriate advice". Her voice started to quiver as she told me she was passing me through to a colleague. I was immediately put through to the bereavement support team. This surprised me – wow, they've got an entire team who deal with this. How many calls does that team get in a day, I wonder?

The lady who answered the phone addressed me personally and efficiently. This is just what I needed and I felt at ease, despite feeling emotional at the words I needed to tell her. I don't want to be saying these words, I don't want it to be true. I was asked for various details from Martha's interim death certificate, which I gave. I'll receive a formal letter in the post to clarify what we've discussed and was advised that the phone contract will be cancelled from today.

One more job done, one more formality dealt with. What do I do once *everything* is dealt with? It's a long way from now, so perhaps by that time I will be further along in my healing, but I don't welcome the day when there's nothing to do.

My home is so quiet now. I sit here and look over at the chair in the corner where she'd often sit, immersed on my laptop or texting her friends. All the washing up is done; I made a half-hearted attempt this morning to put her stuff into some kind of order upstairs. I folded her clean laundry and placed it lovingly in a spare chest of drawers in the upstairs hallway.

I'm tripping over boxes in my bedroom, which contain bundles of her clothing. I try on one of her jackets and can just about get away with it if I don't zip it up fully. I smell the collar and beckon her back to me. Be alive again. Longing for her is now gentle rather than agonising. It needs to become comforting as it's such a natural human instinct under the circumstances.

I picture her in my mind with this jacket on – she looked so elegant in it, she was nearly a woman. Eight weeks ago today it happened; now there are autumn leaves on the pavements, so I've entered a new season without her. I will overcome this, I will beat it. A good friend and I met for breakfast earlier and told me that they're not going abroad for Christmas, which they normally do. I feel so relieved by this – we've spent Christmas together before, so I know I'll be OK now. This is good news and I feel better about looking ahead.

I flicked through some of her school books and read her handwriting. There's also make-up and jewellery, little hand-written notes and sweets. I don't know what to do with a lot of this stuff, so I give up and come back downstairs. I'll face it another time. I don't have the energy right now.

Last night I kept my reservation for the postponed family meal and arranged to meet a friend instead. It was raining heavily and getting dark already when I left home around 6.40pm. The electronic sign at the bus stop indicated fifteen minutes until the next bus, so I started walking. I felt listless and without purpose as I walked. The expanse of road ahead seemed endless as though I was walking on a treadmill. With every step, everything ahead stayed at the same distance and I wondered if I was dreaming.

A car drove past through an enormous puddle and the spray soaked me. It doesn't matter, I thought to myself, I'm not really here anyway. I bumped into neighbours we lived next to about five years ago. They live in Spain now, but still come back to their house in Oxford now and again. They told me they'd heard the news. I felt emotional and didn't say much apart from the odd word. They told me I should come to Spain if I ever want to get away from it all. As they said goodbye they gently patted me on the side of my arm. It was a gesture that silently said so much – pat pat, there there. It was as though they were patting a baby to will it to sleep, being mindful of how fragile it was.

So there we were: Friday night – this is what it looks like – middle-aged divorcees in their little tribes, sitting on bar stools looking wanton. I don't want to be part of this tribe, I never did. I'd usually be at home with my girl, happily looking forward to the weekend together. I'd rarely go out on a Friday night as I loved being with her; we'd cook dinner and watch something on iPlayer, snuggling up together. I'd complain her mass of curly hair was in my face and she'd get annoyed at me. I'd sweep it to the side and she'd squirm away from me in annoyance.

That thought makes me smile now, how much we took one another for granted, but then that's life isn't it? Shouldn't we be able to be a little bit complacent? There's nothing worse than a sycophant who drives you mad with appreciation and unhealthy adoration; a good balance between the two is the answer. Then again human beings are flawed and continually striving to reach a good midpoint. We always need to redress the balance – that's why we go on holiday and our perspective is slightly changed when we get back, because being away has helped us to see that we were getting work, family and life out of sync with each other. Managing all of these factors is tricky to get right a hundred per cent of the time.

# Sunday 15th September: Day 57

I go for my usual Sunday morning coffee with a friend. It's raining and cloudy, the temperature's dropped and I'm feeling shaky. It's OK I say to myself, this is fine. We sit in a café warming our hands with our coffee cups, I'm feeling forlorn and emotional. I don't buy the *Sunday Times* today and decide not to visit Martha at the cemetery. I don't want to and that's just fine, too.

Another friend picks me up and drives me into the city centre. She's arranged for us to attend a lunchtime performance by an ensemble called Azut that her friend is part of. It's held in a large modern basement room within the Ashmolean Museum.

I'm not sure how I'll respond as there's a cello there and the last time I heard cello music was at Martha's funeral. So we sit near the exit just in case I need to make a quick escape. There's also a double bass, accordion, bassoon, clarinet and eight-string electric guitar.

A French guy starts to sing and they all start to play. It sounds a bit like 'Minnie the Moocher' with a French twist; it's jolly and upbeat, so I'm feeling happy rather than melancholy. Between pieces the French guy explains what the next piece is about. I can't really understand a lot of it as he speaks in French with the odd bit of English here and there, but that doesn't detract from the music anyway.

## Sunday 15th September: Day 57

The next piece is instrumental and sounds like a benediction on a Scottish hillside. It's haunting and melodic, but this doesn't strip me bare emotionally either, so I relax. Being here is a good break from the norm, though I'm still in my city so feel safe and comforted. I'm still near my girl but I'm doing different things, new things, and the signs of progress are good.

I look around the room; Oxford people have such a distinct look. Women in their late fifties and early sixties with bobbed hair, an alice band holding it carefully in place. I imagine they married an academic whom they met at university. Bringing up the children took up all of their time, but these women can hold their own around any dinner table. Now the children have left home they do the odd course at The University of Oxford's Department for Continuing Education.

Over the past twenty-three years in Oxford, I've met many clever women whom I can sense are frustrated as they didn't fulfil their own potential. They'd wistfully discuss what they used to be good at and what could have been had their lives taken a different direction. So they sit at this concert alongside me, wearing their pork pie shaped shoes, which are both comfortable and hard-wearing, their heads full of possibilities.

A baby at the back of the room starts to giggle, I glance around and everyone is smiling. This moment is shared and nurtured, the giggling continues and bounds off the strings of the double bass, through the audience, to be taken with us into our lives. The throaty beat of the double base vibrates through my ribcage and into my heart. A precious, invisible moment that makes me feel alive again. This is worth living for, I can still feel happiness. I'm also one of those women who didn't feel as though she'd reached her potential, but since Martha's death turning to my writing has enabled me to change all that.

# Monday 16th September: Day 58

I've just been onto the HMRC website and submitted a form to cancel child benefit for Martha. I have to click through the words 'Your child has died' from a bulleted list. My click through changes the text from blue to lilac. Never would I have thought I would be doing this. I'm on autopilot and don't feel a thing.

I dutifully complete the form. It's a 'general form' and there's no tick box to select that my child has died but there's a box at the bottom with the words 'Please use this space to ask us your question(s)'. I don't have a question; what shall I ask? Perhaps I should say 'How do I do this, please do tell?' Who would do this if I died?

I write in the box 'My child died on 20th July 2013'. Then click the word 'Next'. Yes, indeed I think.

Child benefit is paid until eight weeks beyond the date of death, which is generous. Another stage in this journey ticked off my list. Don't get down that list too eagerly I tell myself, you don't know what's waiting for you at the end of it. I had to include Martha's date of birth on the form; that felt nice – when she was born – a very important date to prove her existence.

She made an impactful impression on this planet, her death has shown that. She was far from perfect, but that makes this even more poignant – people like to relate to others, flaws and all. Martha wasn't a saint, so her flaws help other people, especially her teenage friends, to feel her loss even more acutely.

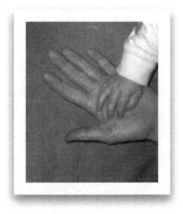

# Tuesday 17th September: Day 59

Yesterday was a good day, in that I felt OK for the majority of the day. I always have the odd moment, but it's more gentle on me now, it doesn't leave me in agony. The pains in my stomach and heart are permanently there, but I'm getting used to them now. They're not welcome, exactly, but I've accepted the pain now, so rather than fighting it out of my system, I'm allowing it to be what it needs to be, and by not focusing on it too much, my mind is pleasantly distracted elsewhere.

I've tried to put thoughts of Martha out of my mind. I'm not trying to deny her, but in order to progress I need to find ways to manage, and by not visualising the terrible things that exist in my memory I'm dismissing those thoughts rather than letting them linger. This has helped me to feel lighter inside. For the same reason I'm also not looking at her photos for too long.

I kind of feel that she's with me now. I'm not a hundred per cent sure, but there's something that's definitely changed since the day of the burial. I'm feeling at peace and there's no explanation for that, but it's calming. Anyway, there's so much about life that's inexplicable that all I can gauge my feelings by is my instincts and they're telling me that all is well and that Martha is at peace too.

## Tuesday 17th September: Day 59

Today is a day that most people would describe as 'miserable' – it's raining heavily and the sky is one big grey-white lid. But that's just peripheral; a bit like being lonely in a crowded room, you need to use mind over matter. Today is as necessary as any other day in my life; every single moment is a moment I'm at the mercy of and I'm welcoming it all in. I'm trying to let the 'bad' be my lesson and the 'good' my reward for that lesson. Some of it doesn't make sense, but I accept it regardless and know that at some point down the road I may unravel the meaning of a particular lesson. Whether I understand all of it or not is immaterial as enough does seep through to wake up my mind.

When you let go of your vulnerability and stop worrying about your fears or what other people think you enter a world full of simplicity. Your head clears and you're able to concentrate on what's really important – your own individual journey. The people we share our lives with are crucial and valid, but it's important to remain focused on what your needs are and what you feel you are here to achieve.

I feel that I'm here to teach and inspire based on my life experiences. I want people to really think about things and I never, ever want them to experience how it feels to be me as this is not how it should be, this is unnatural. I think I'm strong enough to take this – but it's an incredibly arduous path to walk at times. I want people to feel the emotion, passion and empathy in my words as I speak to them. I have a message and that message is that we all need to wake up and stop allowing ourselves to be distracted from what's important in life.

Most of us make decisions based on ego, insecurities or fear. The reality is that worrying is an emotion that has too much dominance over our lives. I'm not saying that it shouldn't feature at all, but it should be much further down our list of priorities than it tends to be.

## Tuesday 17th September: Day 59

Think about it, if you work hard to rid your daily life of worry and fear all your stress and anxiety starts to dissipate. Make decisions based on your gut instinct and stop using the word 'but' … and before you know it you're making positive changes in your life that will lead you onto the right path, to what you're really here to achieve.

How often have you heard yourself or someone else say 'I can't do what I really want to do with my life because … I've got to pay the rent or mortgage / I'm too old now / I have too much to lose / etc.' We've made the choices that we live within the confines of, and of course, circumstances do dictate to an extent, but our gut is always there to remind us of our true purpose: "Hello, this is your gut speaking … you know that you want to retrain to become a [INSERT DREAM JOB], but you're allowing the constraints of your overheads to stop you. But you have a choice, you always have a choice."

Now, I know these things are easier said than done, but think about those moments in your life when you've said, "I've had it" or "I'm not taking this any more", and you visualise in your mind what you want. Now think about what you've got. Your frustration or unhappiness tells you that, no matter how inconvenient or practical this next decision will be, that change needs to happen for you to feel fulfilled and to reach your true potential.

A random conversation may then take place and before you know it you're starting to pave the way for positive change and 'coincidental' and relevant things start to appear in your life because you've had a wake-up call. You take that first brave step and wish you had done it years ago. At least you're doing it now and it's never too late – all very clichéd perhaps, but it's pretty simple really. We over-complicate our lives and the fundamental elements of life are actually a lot less complex than we imagine.

## Tuesday 17th September: Day 59

So dread the winter or try to see beauty and enjoyment within every moment over the coming months – it's up to you. I'm determined to experience this first winter without my precious daughter with contentment in my heart. I have a choice too and now realise that I always did; I'm awake now, it's taken a while but I'm finally awake.

# Wednesday 18th September: Day 60

Throughout every day over the past two months I've said over and over to myself 'this really happened, didn't it?' In my head I was trying to get over the shock of it and at the same time tell myself to accept it because it is true and it did happen. Over the past few days, I've suddenly stopped saying this, so I think I've accepted it now, the shock is waning. I feel I'm taking the first steps towards being free to get on with my own life.

I cooked last night for the very first time since Martha died. I invited over two friends who have helped me so much over the past couple of months. Their gentle temperaments are just what I needed for my first attempt. I went to the shops with a rough idea in my mind of what I could manage at this stage. Walking around the aisles I glanced at items I'd normally buy for her, but I'm no longer upset by these reminders.

I work out a plan in my head and it comes together without any feelings of pressure or concern. Despite the torrential rain outside, I enjoy my slow walk home and this moment, as it is pivotal. I see a bright pink rose covered in raindrops and look at it in wonder. I'm healing, I'm getting better.

The meal is roast vegetables with goat's cheese and beetroot, served with salad and toasted pine kernels. It's simple, but tasty.

## Wednesday 18th September: Day 60

I savour each stage of the preparations; laying the table is a nice, symbolic ritual for this special night. I always used to have friends over for dinner as it enabled me to remain at home with Martha whilst maintaining a social life. I think this is why she was so confident socially and with all age groups.

For me there is no better way to spend time with the people I care about than sitting around a table, sharing a meal. The best times of my life have been spent this way. So this first meal is my first attempt at getting that back into my new life. My friends knew I'd take a cookbook to bed to plan a forthcoming dinner and would always joke with me about this. I really enjoy planning a menu and working out what works with what – I'm not a brilliant cook, but I'm competent and, most importantly, I'm a relaxed host.

My preference in staying at home to entertain isn't exactly the best way to meet a guy, but I've always felt certain that I will meet the right person one day. It's never worried me; I've half-heartedly dabbled with online dating, but apart from paying the initial fee to join for three months or so, I'd rarely log back in, let alone respond to messages, so I wasn't exactly making the most of it.

Under the present circumstances I doubt now is the time for dating, but whoever that may be, he'll need to be incredibly genuine, balanced and understanding. In the meantime, I have work to do and a life to continue living.

I'm sitting in a coffee shop on the Cowley Road in Oxford. I'm visiting a nearby therapist for an hour of craniosacral therapy, which I've been recommended to help me get over the trauma. I've never had this before, but I'm trying anything I can right now, as you never know what may help and I'm very open-minded and willing at the moment. If it eases the pain in my heart, then that would give me some relief.

So I'm taking back my life for myself; I immerse myself in my own needs and I do not apologise for who I am – something I was guilty of in the past. Little did I know then that I was actually putting people off as I was subconsciously saying, "I'm blocked. To enable me to let you in, you need to navigate an obstacle course alongside me and I will then evaluate you and decide whether you're worth the risk as I can't risk being hurt again."

I was overthinking it all, and as I've said before, it's a lot simpler than that. Being open to allow yourself to be loved requires you to be happy in yourself and there's an element of risk-taking involved and a bit of vulnerability too. I get it now.

I'm amazed I'm feeling so healed in just over two months. I don't want to jinx this as I know there are difficult moments ahead, but surely I'm over the worst of it. Surely I can take what's ahead. Fingers crossed that's the truth. I don't want to be taught any more lessons for a while – I need a rest from being thrown in at the deep end.

In the mornings I now wake up and just lie there contentedly and the power of my own self-belief comforts me. I am enough for my life. I'm willing to share my life if that opportunity arises in the future, but this is good; it feels gentle and genuine. As well as observing life, I am taking part in it again. A good balance of the two.

I suspect Martha would have settled down quite young – she needed companionship and was very comfortable with that natural human instinct. She was a tactile girl; when she sat with me she'd unconsciously entwine her hand in mine – at times she'd remember she was annoyed at me for something and would momentarily withdraw her hand, only to unconsciously take my hand again a few moments later. I'd always notice this and smile knowingly.

Human beings are supposed to be paired off, but I've allowed myself to reprogram and the close bond I had with Martha was enough for me. In the present circumstances I need to reprogram myself again and, minus the fear I used to be driven by, my heart is now open completely – it misses the odd beat, but it's never felt so pure and genuine.

Martha taught me so much. I remember when she was about eight and was asking me about my job at the time, which I wasn't really enjoying, she said, "Well get another job then." I told her it's not as easy as that, as I need to earn money to pay our bills, and her reaction was one of disbelief; she said, "You just do your job for the money?" I remember that so clearly and it taught me so much. Although from her childlike viewpoint our circumstances were seen more simplistically, it certainly made me stop and think.

Coming out of her primary school one day she stopped me and gasped. She said, "Look how beautiful it is", and, crouching down to her level to have a look, I saw there was some fungus on a wall, which indeed was very beautiful. She noticed things and retaught me to look at the world with wonder.

She also taught me to believe in that first feeling you get when you meet someone. You get a sense of who they really are, which usually turns out to be true – Martha never swayed from that and wouldn't make much of an effort if she felt someone was less than genuine. This used to embarrass me at times, but she was right to stick to her true instincts regarding the true nature of someone's character.

Despite also having her own insecurities, she demanded her needs vehemently and without compromise. Her head was clear and she wouldn't sway from her requirements, despite my protestations at times. I'd secretly admire her tenacity and determination. This taught me how I should be and that I'd lost my way somewhat. I'd strayed so far from my natural needs and demanded nothing for myself – so that's exactly what I got.

During the craniosacral therapy I mentioned my breathing was shallow despite having tried to moderate this myself, and that I had an intense pain at the base of my sternum. A very lovely girl gently put her hand on the right-hand side of my abdomen; immediately each breath was drawn down further and the natural rhythm extended; I maintained each slow breath without any effort, nothing felt forced. I don't know how she did this, but I was so relieved and felt instantly better. As I left I felt my throat had opened up too, so I decided to walk back into the city centre rather than get the bus. Everything looked more in focus; I'm still a little bit spaced out, but clarity is returning.

I'm walking the same route as Martha walked on the day she died. She walked along this pavement for the final time all those weeks ago, wheeling my bike alongside her. I brush that thought out of my head and distract myself by acknowledging what a lovely afternoon it's turned out to be, despite the rainy morning that welcomed the day. I'm feeling so energised as my breathing is improved, reducing the pain in my chest. I cut through the back streets and pass the Fudge Kitchen with its permanent 'Come in for a free sample' sign outside. Martha had a loyalty card for that place, which is a mystery to me as she only ever went in for the free samples. She was funny like that, she loved a freebie.

I looked through her purse the other day and there were various cards; Boots advantage, a library card and her bank card. At our local bank, we'd gone in together a while back as she wanted to pay in some money that she'd earned from feeding our neighbour's cat. I knew the guy behind the counter and when he served Martha he said, "Martha have you tippexed your name on the signature strip?" And she said, "Yes, because I didn't like how I did it the first time." The queue of people heard and we all laughed. She didn't really understand why this was funny or why it had been brought up in the first place. I need to close that bank account down now. There's nothing in it, but in order to sort out all the formalities and stop getting statements and automated updates, I need to bring in the death certificate and arrange a meeting with them to get this all concluded. I hope they let me keep the card as a memento of that innocent mistake; in the end she just signed it 'martha X'.

# Thursday 19th September: Day 61

Today has been busy, I've felt OK and mainly upbeat. Late in the afternoon, I lie on the sofa for a rest as I needed some time to stop distracting myself to allow what's on my mind to emerge. I seem to have stopped thinking about Martha constantly. As I lie here I feel a little bit down – or is it more than that, is it melancholy? I'm not sure. I am OK, but I do feel a little bit lost. I'm doing well in keeping myself busy and trying to find meaning in my new life, but I have momentary lapses in this as my girl seeps back into my present, and in those moments I don't quite know what to do with myself.

Is this good enough, will I be OK? I cast my mind back and wonder how the hell I'm still standing after what's happened. I somewhat dread what's ahead for me, as I know I can't possibly feel this healed after only eight weeks. I'm not being cynical, but common sense tells me to watch out and remain open-minded with regard to my ongoing recovery. I've barely had space in my mind to grieve over the past couple of months due to the number of difficult decisions I've needed to make.

So, I've had a good day today, another one under my belt without too much pain. I head up to bed and perch on the edge. I glance briefly at myself in the mirror and my face crumples as I start weeping uncontrollably. These emotions are so mixed, I can't really work out what happened in that moment – what did I see? It catches me unawares and it's as though I'm observing someone else. I've never glimpsed myself crying before; I'm strangely curious about it – my face looks so bereft in this moment, my eyes are no longer able to hide my shattered thoughts and diminishing history. It's as though I'm watching a woman crying and trying to console herself – I feel sad and helpless for her, but I know that she needs to have time to herself to respect each individual emotion and to let it pass.

I wonder if being able to visualise it as someone else crying is my way of detaching from the pain. I'm sure it is. I turn the light off and lie down in the darkness, my sobbing reverberating in my ears, my shoulders convulsing with each restricted breath. I cover my eyes with my forearm to will the tears to stop; they trickle through the sides of my eyes and I feel them on my arm and down my face.

I turn the light back on and get a tissue to blow my nose as I can't breathe; I feel helpless and alone. I don't want sympathy, I am not a victim, I do not want anyone to feel sorry for me I can do this, it'll just take time – my thoughts are pragmatic and clear. I slip into a deep and peaceful sleep. Her shadow is in the darkest corner of my room, but as I heal that darkness will comfort rather than haunt me.

# Saturday 21st September: Day 63

Nine weeks on. It's 2.15pm on a Saturday. In my mind I'm back to where I was nine Saturdays ago. It seems like a lifetime. I dispel the vision of her face as it doesn't represent her truly. I can't allow myself to dwell on that image. It's now 2.17pm, the official time that will appear on her final death certificate. She was born at 6.41am and died at 2.17pm – these two times are now forever etched in my mind.

The pain in my heart now feels walnut-sized rather than like a fist. I'm OK with this, it's a sign of progress in the right direction and that's all I can hope for right now. My home is no longer a florist's shop – I've taken all the cards down, apart from a few that I'm still getting from people who've only just heard or who just couldn't find the right words until now.

I boxed up her clothes and shoes this morning. Some for charity, some for her little cousin, and the rest I'll keep until I'm clearer on what to do with them. I put two boxes on top of my wardrobe – I don't think having them looming over me when I'm in bed will have a negative impact on me; I'm trying not to let them anyway. We'll see.

Having cleared the floor space my head immediately feels calm and uncluttered too – such a simple thing has had such a positive effect on me. This is good, I tell myself. I need my space back for myself; I need to pave the way for my own life. I've lived sixty-three days without my girl and I'm still standing. I am really present in every moment and I'm here, fully immersed and eager to have a fulfilled life.

Once you stop yearning and learn to accept it, you kind of stop missing her, as missing her hurts so much. So you block out those thoughts and feelings and use absolute facts in order to keep going. I've accepted her death as I accepted her life. I've now accepted both of those within my present circumstances and this is necessary and healthy.

I look out of the window and see a white feather floating in the wind – no – it's a delicate white butterfly highlighted by the distant grey-blue clouds. Whether it's false meaning or hope, it makes me smile even from a face which feels as though it's dragging down and hanging off my skull. Being able to smile is pretty incredible under the circumstances, but I genuinely feel happy, and feel like smiling at times, and this re-energises me and makes me think that my recovery is beginning.

# Sunday 22nd September: Day 64

I found it difficult to get to sleep last night; I felt a bit scared for the first time. I'm not normally scared of the dark, but as I lay there I heard noises and my imagination ran away with itself. I thought I heard intruders – they can take whatever they want, I thought to myself.

Over the past few weeks it's as though intruders have taken over my head and they've only recently left. I've now cleared up the trail of mess they left behind and have changed the locks. Only remnants of memories left now, nothing tangible. I sigh with relief.

I've grown up a lot over the past few weeks. It's not that I wasn't grown up before, it's just that I'm now taking myself more seriously (although not too seriously). I will no longer allow other people's dreams to distract me from mine, or be so passive in the future. My path is *my* path. Other people will form paths alongside mine – we'll journey together at times and maybe forever, but my path is still my path and my true purpose is what I must remain focused on.

This morning I rolled my yoga mat out for the first time since Martha died. That balance you get within yoga practice tells you a lot about what emotions you're feeling inside. Yoga is so important to me, it helps me to stretch away the stresses life leaves on my body – a cricked neck, a sore back from sitting at a desk, all alleviated by the practice of yoga.

I take it gently as I'm still fragile, but now my breathing is moderated I have the strength to try it. Like the grieving process, it'll take time for me to reach a point where my mind is elevated by regular yoga practice. You can't do any of the more advanced moves properly until you've given the easier moves the respect they deserve. But I'm happy to have reached this point in my recovery – it's a good sign.

I decide to do my Sunday morning routine alone today; I'm feeling emotionally ready to tackle it alone. So I buy the *Sunday Times* and go to a local café for coffee. They're playing great music, which lifts my spirits. I sit happily, flicking through 'Style' magazine, and feel empowered by being happy alone again. I watch a couple with their baby girl and smile to myself; this no longer fills me with remorse or sadness. I'm a single woman again and I'm happy with that. I don't yearn, I don't torture myself by needing the physical Martha to be in my new life and I don't feel guilty about this.

I'll always be a mother, I'll always be her mum and I'm proud of that. But my new circumstances have forced me to reinvent myself and how I think about my life and of myself. I need to be enough for my life, I now say to myself – I am enough. My new mantra is both healthy and progressive.

I visit the cemetery with a couple of old friends who I hadn't seen since the funeral. I've never seen it so busy, cars parked all along the driveway, numerous little groups huddled around plots holding bunches of flowers or looking wistful and longing. I light a tealight and put it in the lantern some friends bought the other day. I notice some of Martha's friends have been to visit and left flowers and little notes. It cheers me up to think that other people visit her and take the time to pay their respects.

When you bury a loved one, you never know whether you'll ever want to visit the cemetery again, or regularly attend to it. Neither scenario is wrong, but I've found it comforting and grounding. At the back of my mind, I realise that I'm also visiting my own future grave and that fact spurs me to make the most of the life I have left.

I discuss what to do when all the flowers wilt and talk about my idea of creating a beach scene. I also think about buying some beautiful artificial flowers as you can get some nice ones these days; that way she can have a beautiful colourful plot all year round. What would Martha like? I wonder; she'd probably want graffiti art or something funny, although I think she'd like the beach scene idea as it links well with our perfect last day together.

I hope I can travel again one day without my perfect little travel companion, without feeling bereft. It would be a shame not to continue exploring the world as there's so much adventure left in me. Like my yoga practice, I'll just need to ease myself in gently and start with little daytrips in order to gauge whether I'm ready yet to do anything further afield.

She'd want that for me; she had so much adventure left in her when she died, so many plans and potential. I'll need to live my life with the zest of her spirit, using the wonderful memories we shared and knowing that that's the way it should be. Regardless of where I am in the world, the memories are carried within me. My home doesn't have to be a physical place, it can be within my mind and heart. I'm feeling less lost now, less abandoned. I am one tiny person in this universe; I am but a minute particle in the scheme of this enormous world. I am enough for my life now, I am enough.

# Monday 23rd September: Day 65

I grab her dressing gown and breathe in the sweet scent as I walk down the stairs to shower. I wrap my arms around it and pretend it's her. As I lay in bed this morning I felt flat. When does everything start to come together again? Can I truly survive this, can I ever be free of the burden?

I'm emotional today – it's bearing down on me. This load is heavy and my knees give as I'm too weak. When I manage to get through an entire day without feeling overwhelmed by this burden, I wonder if I'm through it but I also question this feeling as it'd be unnatural to be over it so soon.

But being immersed in every single moment does make me feel the feeling within that moment so fully that I almost forget that I can feel any other way. I'm truly grounded, fully rooted in the earth; it's nice to feel so 'right now', not planning too far ahead and not going over yesterday too much either – just fully in the here and now.

I'm here for what seems like forever and she's not here – forever. It's a burden and it's messing with my head and depriving me of the future I was prepared for. I feel robbed: robbed of my daughter, robbed of a son-in-law, robbed of my future grandchildren, robbed of the natural pattern of my life.

## Monday 23rd September: Day 65

Half a gram of powder robbed me of all of this. My daughter took it to enhance her senses and make her feel even happier than she was already. 'If only' eats away at my insides, acid simmering, obliterating the porridge I ate for breakfast this morning and leaving my body eating itself.

I look out of the window and see a Virgin air balloon nearby. It slowly lifts through the clouds like an apparition, disappearing through the fog to reappear again a few seconds later, coming back under the cloud cover. My life feels as though I'm a passenger on that balloon – I have an element of control, but mostly I've got to accept that other factors dictate my course and destiny.

# Saturday 28th September: Day 70

These past few days have been gentler, more manageable. When I think of her now it doesn't rip me apart emotionally; it's as though she is a sense or a feeling, rather than a physical person now. It's odd, but interesting, how you get to this point after so many years together.

I've had to force myself to compartmentalise my thoughts and feelings as it's too much to contend with if I don't. Making plans for any night of the week without considering Martha's needs doesn't now leave me feeling bereft or reluctant to venture on to new pastures. I'm enjoying my freedom by changing my routine quite significantly. There are fewer reminders on these nights out now as most of the places are new to me.

The sadness lies languidly in the pit of my stomach and probably always will. I carry it around but refuse to allow it to weigh me down. It's heavy, but I'm determined to build my strength and fight on.

I no longer feel a constant urge to talk about her, but don't feel that I can't either – when the moment takes me, I talk openly about her. People don't die if they live on the lips of the living. My friends talk fondly of her too and this gladdens my heart as I can sense the love they feel for her. They recognise how important it is for me to keep her with us; they cherish their own memories of her and we share them generously. It's important to be able to express these feelings, rather than reach a point where it's awkward or viewed as inappropriate or distasteful.

So I now have ten weeks of my own personal new history as a lone woman and that's OK. Even over the past fortnight I've noticed a difference: I feel stronger and slightly healed. My home has never been tidier; my walking pace and the pace at which I cycle have all slowed down. I no longer rush around manically as I used to. The pace of my pedalling on my bike is now a meandering rate, rather than thigh-burningly fast. Martha and I would walk ridiculously quickly, only realising this when we had company.

So I cycle along softly, and intently turn the pedals. Admittedly I'm a lot weaker and my strength needs to increase, but it feels great to pedal around this lovely city again. Autumn is here, the trees are a muted technicolour – Martha's hair comes to mind – tones of brown, copper and gold. With each mild breeze, a flurry of leaves descends to the ground below. The cycle of the seasons, the cycle of life. Quiet statements declaring that change is constant and we must move with it. I am, I think to myself, I am.

The other night I went to the cinema for the first time 'since'. It was OK, I didn't have an emotional meltdown. Another first: see, you can do this, I think. I had pre-bought tickets to take her to the cinema to see the new Simon Pegg film, *The World's End* on 21st July. But my world temporarily ended the day before instead.

As I snuggled into the cinema seat, the darkness felt safe and familiar. My lovely friend sat with me and I didn't allow my mind to dwell on how many times Martha and I had shared moments like this. No, I say to myself, don't do that, you are right here, right now. This moment counts, it really, really does.

# Saturday 5th October: Day 77

'Doing' now seems to come at such a price. 'Doing' before was dutiful, worrying at times, but truly led by expected milestones and future achievements, and it was also a more natural path. 'Doing' now, well, I sometimes just don't know what to 'do' with myself. I'm keeping busy 'doing' interesting things, I ensure the routine is varied to stave off malaise, surround myself with good people and allow myself enough time alone to gather my thoughts and face my grief in private. Despite all this I'm left feeling truly disorientated in both the cold light of day and within the confines of darkness.

A couple of days ago 'doing' was challenging from the very second my conscious mind realised I was awake. Right, what have you got for me today? I thought. I met a friend and we took her dog for a walk. A sense of foreboding pushed against me throughout our walk, like a strong wind I was facing and struggling to contend with. Rest stops helped, but the invisible barrier exasperated me and I found myself panicking and giving in to it.

OK grief, let's work together; you pushing against me will ultimately make me stronger. I'll have to rest at times, but I'll never lie down and surrender. I come so close though to giving in at times, as it shakes me so vigorously – it's the same as the feeling you get when you come off the waltzer at the fair. 'Scream if you want to go faster': no, I think I'll get off now. The thrills are too much for me and I need to plant my feet on firm ground and have clarity again.

I use my mature internal voice to console and keep myself going: 'Come on, you can do this' or 'You're doing so well, look how far you've come', it says. But that's all very rational and logical and this reality isn't. Eleven weeks ago today ... and I'm feeling so emotionally sober, my thoughts are rattling around in my head trying to file themselves. Shall we file ourselves under 'aftershock' or 'partially recovered'?

The clarity I've had over the past few weeks now seems jumbled and confusing. I'm tired, mostly, not exhausted like I was in the beginning, but due to the circumstances of Martha's death, there's so much additional stuff to contend with. We're still waiting for the final pathology tests and report to be drawn up, then the criminal side of things to be decided upon, as well as the coroner's hearing to determine the actual cause of death.

The added stress all this has caused has swept my focus away from grieving, so at times the grief leaps onto my shoulders, covers my eyes and shouts, "Remember me, don't ignore me, you can't hide from me – ever". I lose my footing and try not to fall over, my breathing is irregular. I truly respect the grief, I must face it squarely and with grace. I reply weakly, "I know I can't hide from you, you're always there, but I have all this other stuff to sort out, so I need to put you aside."

If I'm honest, I'd ignore the grief until my dying day. I'd squash it into a suitcase weighed down by bricks and throw it in the canal. Blissful ignorance is what I want; let's play dress-up and pretend – I'll play the mummy and you be the baby and we all live happily ever after. Yes, that's what I want, that's what we all want. Some are lucky enough to achieve that and some aren't, so there. Who's the winner?

Even before this happened, I never took anything for granted (apart from my roughly imagined and anticipated future I suppose); I wasn't a complacent person. Small mercies were appreciated and acknowledged, and a 'feet on the ground' approach was prevalent in my life, as was a determination to give something back to the world and respond to those issues Martha and I cared deeply about.

So here I am, seventy-seven days on. I don't want to keep measuring or analysing, but find myself curiously fascinated by timelines and evaluation. I've realised that on Martha's sixteenth birthday, which is on 30th October, she'll have been dead for 102 days. What a centenary. As of today, I've lived for 15,618 days – that's 9,876 more than Martha did. She lived for 820 weeks and I've lived for 2,231 weeks – it really doesn't sound like much, but her 820 weeks sounds like nothing at all.

The time I devoted to caring for Martha now seems like a blur – a snippet rationed to me, and I had no idea that it would end so prematurely. The time I now have seems endless and is echoing around me; I'm lost in this emptiness. I stretch my arms out and reach for a stable surface to steady myself, but am welcomed by a void, so I must find this steadiness within myself.

You can never replace the one you lost, it's a truly impossible task. So I fill my time up, full to the brim. It cascades over the top and I stare at the mess on the floor with disdain. See, that's what a full life can look like under my circumstances. It's too much to contend with; a full and happy life ahead seems daunting and unnatural to me now. The thing most people strive and hope for is the opposite to what would comfort me.

I'm swimming upriver as everyone else is swimming down; I'm fighting the current and my skin is bruising as they all bump past. I'm not like you guys, I think, you all have different goals from me; mine are unnatural and obscure. I hear a distant voice, it's my emotionally sober self saying that I mustn't detach myself from everyone; they've all had things to contend with too, so don't isolate yourself as everybody has different goals, needs and desires.

Yes, I think, but how do I fit mine in with theirs? How can my unnatural life possibly run alongside their more natural lives? I think of magnets that repel one another – no matter how much you try to push them together, it's impossible; but turn them around and suddenly they're attracted and pulled together. Some will stick and others won't – that's how it's always been and that's how it will always be. It's no different really now; yes, my circumstances can make it difficult for me to relate to others, or for others to relate to me, but that depends on what I'm focusing on at the time.

I had started teaching Martha to celebrate the differences between herself and her friends, rather than it always being about similarities. She'd get frustrated at times when her friends didn't get her point of view, and I'd explain that their opinions are important to them and are just as valid. Whether they agreed or not was immaterial as it's good to respect different viewpoints, rather than think that yours is the only opinion that matters. She understood and I could tell that she'd listened to my advice, so I'm using my own advice now and I am listening intently.

# Tuesday 8th October: Day 80

There's no name for someone like me. I'm not able to sum up my circumstances succinctly in one simple word. Surely there must be more 'me's around. I'd like to think there aren't too many though, as that would be a discomfiting thought too.

I'm not a widow or a divorcee. What could you call a single mother who has lost her only child? A widow as defined on Wikipedia is a woman whose spouse has died; a widower is a man. The term widowhood and the word viduity are also used, the latter meaning the state of widowhood for either sex.

When a woman's husband dies she is still married to him even though she is a widow; in the same way, I am still a mother. So the lack of a single word to describe me leaves me having to explain using a whole sentence. By the end of the explanation you can see the colour drain from the face of the person you're talking to – it's too horrific for them to digest and perhaps this is why no such word exists. Perhaps we don't want to face such a horror, therefore we stick our fingers in our ears and say 'la la la', rather than come up with an appropriate word.

I click through to the history of single parents and am taken to this:

HISTORY

Single parenthood has been common historically due
to high parental mortality rate (due to disease, wars and
maternal mortality). Historical estimates indicate that in
French, English, or Spanish villages in the 17th and 18th
centuries at least one-third of children lost one of their
parents during childhood; in 19th century Milan about half
of all children lost at least one parent by age 20; in 19th
century China almost one-third of boys had lost one parent
or both by age 15. Divorce was generally rare historically
(although this depends by culture and era), and divorce
especially became very difficult to obtain after the fall of
the Roman Empire, in Medieval Europe, due to strong
involvement of ecclesiastical courts in family life (though
annulment and other forms of separation were more
common).

I email a friend to explain my dilemma and he sends me a link
to a discussion on a WordReference forum on this exact subject.
People from all over the world have commented on whether a
word exists in their culture for this purpose or not. We know
there isn't such a word in English, and simply refer generically to
a bereaved parent, and there doesn't seem to be such a word in
Portuguese either. In Germany, they don't have a single word, but
say 'verwaiste Eltern' (which literally means orphaned parents).
According to the forum the nearest seem to be in Hebrew and
Arabic as follows:

> In Hebrew we have הורים שכולים. This says 'horim shakulim' –
> horim means parents.
> אב שכול says 'av shakul' – a father who's lost a child.
> אם שכולה says 'em shakula' – a mother who has lost a child.
> משפחה שכולה says 'mishpakha shakula' – a family who have
> lost a child.

There is also a word for children who have lost their parents
– but it does not mean 'orphan' (orphan is סותי – 'yatom' –
sg. masculine).
The dictionary says לוכש (shkhol) is 'bereavement' –
suffering the loss of a loved person.
In Israel we usually use it when we speak of people losing
their loved ones in the military – as soldiers or in bombings
(in the military we usually speak of people who lost their
children).

Therefore, I suppose many individuals above could be described
as orphans or within the confines of widowhood, but there isn't a
word for my situation.

So I'm a bereaved single parent who has lost her only child. Nine
words rather than one simple one to immediately inform people
what I'm suffering from. I want one word only. One word to
indicate my personal circumstances and the feminine, denoting
the loss of an only child and daughter. The word widow demands
instant respect with no further painful explanation required –
the very second this word is emitted, the listener is clear as to its
meaning. My more wordy explanation leaves them shattered and
bewildered as the words amass and their full horror is revealed.
They don't know how to digest this; their own mortality and that
of their children flashes through their heads and shows behind
their teary eyes. Their voices break and they truly are unable to
find any words, so I get part words. Broken and unfinished words
are attempted, but rarely fully delivered – thrown into the valley
of broken words, unfinished conversations and shattered dreams.

So I'm scavenging through that valley for bits of words to glue
together to form a concise and clear meaning. I find rusty, old
and discarded remnants of letters and try to fit them together
and come up with 'smothered': s to explain that I'm a single
mother and ed for **expired daughter**, but it doesn't work at all,

does it? It's a good way to describe how I feel most of the time, though: I feel smothered by the grief and by the love I still have for Martha.

That's another thing: I never say *loved* her, I always say *love* her. I will never refer to my love for her in the past tense as her death doesn't denote an end to my love; it is infinite as is the stockpile of memories I have of her. So I'm smothered: "Hello, I'm Anne-Marie, and I recently became smothered." "Oh," I hear you say, "how unfortunate. I know exactly what that means."

# Wednesday 9th October: Day 81

I bought a visitors book for Martha's grave today, as when
I arrived last weekend all the candles were lit already and I
was curious about who had been. Although I like the mystery
of it, my curious side led me to buy this book to see what
serendipity lay beyond today. It fills me with pride when friends
independently visit Martha's grave. I'm so grateful to have friends
who take time out of their own lives to care enough, and I'm also
proud of the impact my girl's life had on so many.

A friend and I plant some snowdrops to ensure Martha gets
seasonal flowers in the dead of winter. There are alliums, tulips
and spring bulbs too. It felt incredibly nurturing to do this. I
know you're not here sweetheart, I thought, but doing something
for us both again feels so wholesome. There's no harm in this.
I'm finding my way and there are no rules and I like that.

I've started researching headstones. There's one I've found which
is very simple, like a big pebble with rounded edges and smooth
to the touch. I check the website and notice that commissions
start from £2,700. I knew they cost a fair bit, but I had no idea
they'd be that expensive. Anyway, there's no rush as the soil
needs between six and twelve months to settle before this can be
done, so I'll worry about that later.

We're organising a sixteenth birthday party for her on 30th October, in Freud Café in Jericho. It's an old church, so there's a vast space to fill with all her friends from school and my nearest and dearest. The light filtering through the stained-glass windows creates a mysterious and mesmerising scene which will work well in order to celebrate such a wonderful and quirky young life. One of her favourite bands, Little Comets, has agreed to pre-record her three favourite songs and dedicate them to her so we can show that on the day, and some of her friends want to sing, read poetry or share their memories, so I'm sure it'll be incredible.

The day will begin at 6.41am. To denote the time she was born we're setting off sixteen white floating lanterns at the lake where she died. Then everyone is invited for a big breakfast at the restaurant she was supposed to be doing work experience at this week.

She was going to be waitressing and was really looking forward to it. She'd already started referring to the owner as her boss, which he was bemused by. So I went along for lunch yesterday with a friend and thought about what could have been. I wonder how she'd have got on, as she wasn't exactly the most compliant little character, but perhaps she'd have grown up a bit with this experience under her belt. No doubt she'd have come back with a few hilarious stories and grievances. We'll never really know, but it was nice to think of her there and I'll always associate it with her a little bit now.

So there's lots to distract me and keep busy with. I know I must allow space to grieve, but I've noticed that every four days or so the grief grips me so I can never ignore it for too long. It's daunting to think that's how it is before it's even happened to me as within the confines of the gripping agony, I reel and struggle to contend with it. Although the only way I can measure it by is by thinking back over the past few weeks and knowing that to be sitting here now is a good sign of progress and an acknowledgement of how strong I am.

I'm really looking forward to seeing the bulbs we planted when they flower. I refuse to wish my life away these days as I choose to live in the very moment I'm in, but it's understandable to be wondering what will be going on in my life by then. What will I be thinking? Will it all feel easier?

By then, I'll have experienced my first Christmas and my own birthday without her being physically here. With each of those annual events, I'll no doubt equip myself with new skills and coping mechanisms and breathe a sigh of relief having marked those milestones.

What would she say to me now? I wonder. She'd probably say something funny like, "You're saving a fortune not having to buy so much milk", or perhaps she'd just say that we shared something truly special during the time we had together and weren't we lucky to have had that at least?

# Friday 11th October: Day 83

I kept a friend company yesterday as she sold some of her vintage clothes on a market stall in town. It was twelve degrees and windy, so we were shuffling from foot to foot to keep warm all day. As I cycled in to meet her every whisper of wind sent golden leaves and conker husks to the pavement; my bike slipped slightly sideways on the cycle path as my wheels ploughed through piles of autumnal debris.

Every bump made me shudder and I felt as though a piece of me peeled away and fell to the ground. I'm raw and vulnerable. I cycle slowly now – no need to hurry these days, I'm in no hurry to face the emptiness. Forty-two years old and how many years ahead of me with this to carry? I feel on the verge of falling to pieces, I miss my girl and don't know how not to.

My mother visited a few days ago and mentioned that she'll never forget the look on my face when the curtain at the A&E department was pulled aside. I think she still sees that when she looks at me now; she averts her gaze and our conversations dance around the shadows of those dark memories. She told me that I kept shouting, "I'm not a mum anymore". What a legacy for her to carry in her memory. I don't want to be me, I don't want to be the girl who can trump most bad news stories and send people's heads towards madness.

## Friday 11th October: Day 83

My head is confused; I feel drunk although I'm stone-cold sober. I'm not feeling logical – it's as though a minute membrane is separating the 'complete and utter madness' that no one can return from, from 'sanity' and I'm swaying between the two. Throw a dice and decide – they're both alluring in different ways.

I wrote only once last week, as I needed to rest my head and not think so hard. People ask if I'm working and I wonder if they really 'get it'. Seriously, I think. But I have work to do, that is for sure. My new work will be raising awareness and inspiring teenagers to ensure they're safeguarded within this unregulated industry.

To my dying day I will work tirelessly; that is who I am, I like to 'do'. Writing this book began within hours of Martha's death. This is also my work. It gets it all out of me and perhaps it'll touch and inspire others – that would be a good outcome to all of this. I would be really happy if that happens.

So I've reclaimed myself from the lost and found depot and have returned myself to my rightful owner. Open the suitcase and see what's inside, but do it slowly, a little bit at a time; you can't deal with the contents all in one go as that would be too much. Slip your hand inside and slowly pull out each item, little by little. The tiniest bit of fluff becomes fascinating under these circumstances, a sign of life. I now think in the 'before' and 'after'. My very own BC and AD.

I'm forensic in my thoughts: what did we have for dinner two nights before she died? I can't remember, but keep trying to and don't know why it matters to me. Her last proper meal the night before was Spanish tapas … , thoughts upon thoughts, upon thoughts. That last perfect day at the beach sits like a picture postcard in my head as I read the writing inscribed on it: "Having a wonderful time – wish you were here!" I return to that day, like a safe place in my head, and I can still feel the warm breeze on my face. My girl was still safely by my side that day.

I haven't cried for five days – that's OK. No need to monitor that too closely or read too much meaning into it, but yesterday, standing on that market stall, I felt spaced out and detached from life. People swept past and I looked busy, and was polite when the moment demanded it, but I'm mostly closed off as I must protect myself from random questioning. I'm not ready for strangers to ask me anything that'll make me say those words.

I avoid and I face, I hide and I charge ahead with determination. I'm strong, but my bones feel as though they're made of crystal. I could shatter at any moment; my bones would snap with the wrong question, from the wrong person: "Do you have children?" ... So I take each step so, so carefully. Nothing too strenuous or demanding. There, there, I say to myself, rock a bye baby, pat, pat.

We had our first family meal out the other night, postponed from a few weeks ago. It was OK, enjoyable, not sad at all. So that was hopeful. My family watching to gauge me – is she OK? They seemed relieved that I was laughing and chatting away like my old self.

The child bereavement counsellor said I should enjoy the good days as the bad days will come. So I do – I really, really do. Every second is cherished and fully appreciated. Nothing is taken for granted; there's no room for complacency for fear of reprisals. I must breathe everything in and let it nourish good and kind thoughts. Then I will be all fixed up – heal me, but hurry up about it as I have work to do and adventures to have. Tick, tick, one step closer to the healed me.

But 'you', grief, are still here, looming over me. Can you go away please, or if you must stay, can you at least make yourself useful and stick the kettle on? Or just be quiet please, stop knocking me off balance with your emotional surprises – boo, there you are again. I shudder, my head is too full because of you shocking me all the time – lift the lid and empty my head out. Aaahhh, that feels so much better – nice and light.

As I made my way to bed last night the tears decided that now was a good time. So out they flowed. My face remained still, I let them fall – I wasn't convulsing, I was emotionless apart from the tears. Dear little Martha, I miss you so. I can smell you on your dressing gown and on the inside collar of your winter jacket – your actual smell – isn't that fact bizarre and amazing. You lie in your grave and your smell is here at home embedded in your clothes and bringing madness and comfort to me.

It'd be interesting if tears were in different colours to denote why you're crying: red for bereavement; blue for a broken heart; green for joy etc. A rainbow of emotions, drip, drip – red one minute, green the next; tears breaking out and cleansing me, their bid for freedom from this crippled soul. I imagine them falling and evaporating; the sun shines and the moisture is drawn up into the sky, rainbow clouds appear and rainbow showers fall to water our gardens. These colourful rivers cascade, carving through the mud and land, leaving us mesmerised in their wake.

The river is still now; dark shadows appear, then sharp shards of white light. My eyes cast over this scene, looking for hope and rainbows. The current lurks beneath and a ripple appears on the surface; a long arrow of water moves along, settling downriver. I throw a stone in – plop, splash, a small circle becomes a large circle as it stretches to the full extent of the weight of the stone. I did that; the still water can be affected. One person can throw a stone and start the ripple of change and I will.

# Sunday 13th October: Day 85

I feel a constriction at the depths of my throat, around my trachea. I hear myself gasping out loud, each breath saying, "Keep it together, don't fall to pieces today". It's raining heavily outside this Sunday morning. What do I do with this? The struggle I don't want. The struggle that wants me so badly that it fights to hang onto me, like an ex-boyfriend who won't accept that it's over.

It closes around me and compresses, I'm on the verge. On the verge of what, I don't know, but I'm jumpy today and I feel shivery and tired. "Boo!" and I hear the sound of glass shattering – that's me, a jigsaw on the pavement; fragments, a half eyeball here, two pieces are still partly attached. You can make out the faint image of a heart valve still opening and closing, fighting to keep me here.

I phone a friend who says she'll come and take me out somewhere. I feel a calmness descend, I'm OK again. The constriction has now moved to the base of my sternum. It sits there and snuggles in, making itself comfortable: I'm here for the long haul, it rasps.

I scrub the kitchen sink. The methodical motion of this sets my breathing back to a steady pace: scrub, scrub, there, there, pat,

pat. Tomorrow family from Scotland are coming to stay for a few days – this is good, plans are good. But I need to get 'there' from 'here' and there are many seconds I reluctantly have to live through until that point: 24 hours consist of 86,400 seconds, tick, tick, breathe, breathe, sigh, relief, calmness, thank you.

Steady again, I close my eyes and hang my head back, a long breath. That long breath says forty-two years done. In 2013, in the UK, the average life expectancy for a woman is 85.6; based on that average, I've got 43.6 years to go. Oh joy. I'm in prison and need to serve my sentence until I can be released out into the real world again. Any parole application will be instantly rejected – no way, you need to do your time missy, no shortcuts for you.

My friend arrives to take me out and asks if I want to visit Martha, which I do. We drive up through the heavy rain to the cemetery, which is only five minutes from my home. As we arrive I notice that the candle in the lantern is lit and my heart jumps, it makes me feel so joyful to know she's had visitors today. I notice new flowers, a plant and a couple of letters too. As I crouch to read the writing, two more friends pull up in their car – I'm gleeful now. The positive affect this has on me is evident; they want to visit her and I am incredibly grateful that they take the time out to do this. They love her too.

A few days ago I took the majority of her photos down; her eyes were everywhere and with each subconscious glimpse I died a little bit more. I've started reminding myself again that it really did happen. I stand by her grave and say to myself, this really did happen – how much more evidence do I need? My heart rejects the truth. Please accept it, the truth hurts but through the hurt my future lies, so take me there quick and stop asking so many questions.

Having fewer photos around helps to not inflict this added hurt on myself, but I'm now missing her photos along with missing her. I try anything to see what helps; I float along and say yes to invites and to things I'd normally decline because one of these things may help me. It's tempting to stay at home and curl up, but I force myself to keep planning ahead and to not cancel plans.

It does work; these plans force me to keep a routine, although I'm actually not forcing myself whatsoever – I'm gently going along with everything and at any point when I feel it's too much I just say so and that works out fine. I am really enjoying my independence; my new life is incredibly simple; a pint of milk goes down at the rate of two cups of tea's worth per day, a mere inch of milk every day or two.

Food shopping barely features in my new life. I used to get stressed about feeding my girl due to her tiny appetite. I was always concerned about this – my mind was consumed by ensuring she was fed. "What do you want for dinner?" I'd ask. "I don't mind", she'd say, but she always did. She'd taste something and say suspiciously, "Does this have fennel in it?" I'd get annoyed at how fussy she'd become, despite having been the toddler who ate everything. But lately she'd put her fork down if there was a whisper of an ingredient that she wasn't that keen on, saying "I'll eat it later." But she never did. She'd happily run on fumes rather than let a mushroom pass her lips.

I really don't miss that, so that's another one for the positive list. Focus on the positives: she'll never get old, she'll never suffer from a broken heart, she'll never experience the pain of my death … Yeah, yeah. I try to convince myself, but dying an average of 69.7 years before your time isn't positive. The negatives outweigh the positives in this instance and it's unrealistic to pretend otherwise.

Early in the evening, some friends and I have dinner together. They've brought along their son who is nearly three. As we're passed a glass of wine, he asks if he can have a grown up drink to make him burp and we all laugh at this. Toddlers are so frank and straightforward. I'm getting great joy from spending time with my friends' children. I listen to them intently; I have a very different perspective on them now. I have endless patience and am fascinated by how precious they are. I feel no resentment or jealousy, I'm truly happy for them.

The day ends well. I feel so different from how I did this morning; lightness has returned and I'm feeling less constrained now. Will 'struggle' put its hands around my throat and hold on for too long next time? Will I have the strength to fight back? Yes, I think so, but who knows for sure. As I lie in bed I say thanks – today has been a good day, a really good day.

# Friday 18th October: Day 90

I feel as though I'm in a waiting room in my life, I'm fidgeting in the chair and eager for the door to be opened and my name to be called. Will they mispronounce my surname as usual, or realise that the 'ck' is silent? I swing between feeling determined to get on with things and bewilderment as to what I'm actually doing and what's ahead. I've told family that I'm spending Christmas with friends as I don't think I'll be able to handle a traditional approach this year. Excited children, presents, Christmas cheer and time off work do not feature on my current agenda. I'm not going to turn into Scrooge and become a party pooper, but I'd just like this first one to pass gently and be lightly acknowledged.

Constant contemplation and momentary recognition of the haziness I'm still feeling sends me into a dreamlike state. My relatives left this morning to return to Scotland. Whilst they were here I felt sad, whilst happy to have them around. I'm trying hard to plod onwards without dragging anyone around me down. Yesterday I had a couple of moments when I was on the verge of breaking down, but I held it together to save them from any distress. I'm sure they wouldn't have minded, but I felt it was better to quickly compose myself and carry on regardless.

We went to my parents' for dinner last night. I was bracing myself for a fail as I walked in and the memories of Martha's visits flashed through my head. I thought of our last family dinner around the table we will eat at again tonight – she sat in the right-hand corner, I can still picture her there. Then I see my former self lying on the sofa like a shroud having come here after my darkest moment, at the hospital. I stop my head from doing this: no, stop, be here, be in the right now. Today is new.

Although there were a few sad moments, it was a great night – see, it's not so bad is it? I'm tired, which doesn't help, but I'm OK, we all seem OK. This is how it will be now. As we reverse the car out of the driveway, I wave a weary wave. Her little legs aren't beside me in the car, her hands with their bitten down nails aren't in mine, but I'm OK. I have a non-physical relationship with her now; this is healthy in order to move on, gently. She is non-physical and I'm getting used to that fact.

The ramifications of holding the emotion of yesterday in seep through into my morning. I meet some close friends in a café and find myself shaken and tired. I sniff back the tears as their kind words penetrate my insufficient armour. I'm reluctant to hijack every conversation and steer it to my situation. I'm mindful to also ask how they're doing and to really listen and engage with what they tell me; I am really interested in what else is going on in life, but my tears inevitably force the discussion my way.

After a few minutes I'm OK again, it's out and it needed to be. I drink some water and joke that I'm topping up my tear-bank as it's running low, and that's exactly how it feels. So am I in a waiting room of my life, or is this period my actual life? That's entirely up to me, I suppose. I hear footsteps in the corridor, the door creaks open and they call my name: "Miss Cockburn". I cringe as my name is mispronounced; do I correct them, or leave them in blissful ignorance? Well, just as in everyday life, how you respond depends on what mood you're in. Today I'll be nice and not correct them. I walk down the corridor behind them in silence, quietly contemplating what could possibly lie ahead.

# Monday 21st October: Day 93

For the past few days I've felt a new-found strength, combined with a strange indifference. It's peculiar, but I'm feeling as though I've stepped outside the bubble I've been in for the past few months; I'm no longer floating around and observing life from afar. There's a revived determination too – I'm feeling positive and at times wonder if this is for real as it seems too good to be true.

There's no way to be sure whether this is a permanent state or nature's way of protecting me from what's ahead, but time will tell. Over the past few days I've felt genuine happiness, strength and a sense of freedom from the pain. I'm slightly detached from it. I'm consumed with organising my life, sorting through paperwork, packing boxes of photographs and more of Martha's belongings and tucking them away until I reach a stage at which I'm feeling more certain as to what I want to do with them.

I received some photos last night from the party that was held after the funeral. On the day I was so zoned in to my last moments with my daughter and that serenity prevented me from observing what was going on around me. The photos provided me with images of family and friends as they watched the film of Martha we'd put together. Their faces were crumpled and distraught; some managed meek smiles whilst wiping away their tears. Their own hopes and recognition of Martha's potential were evident, and seeing their pain caused me to weep momentarily for them and for myself.

In the crowd I can see my own face; one photo shows me on the verge of falling to pieces, another shows me smiling with pride. I'm composed and daydreamy, but you can see in my eyes that I'm also lost and bewildered. I'd put so much love and detail into that day, I was exhausted but incredibly relieved that it went so well.

A montage of photos had also been put together, which flashed up from the projector throughout that afternoon, many of which I'd never seen before. They show Martha modelling in woodland and fields; they were surreal and incredibly beautiful, what an interesting girl she was. So full of … yes, that's the thing, we can all have our own version of what she was, who she was. That's quite nice, she certainly wasn't boring.

Thoughts of her potential inflict sadness and pain, so I stop them. I try not to think back too much, but flash, flash, flash, goes my mind. Sweep them aside and carry on; now, right now, right here, that's the only moment that exists. My life is important. That's what I do, that's how I'm getting through this, as well as using writing as a medicinal release.

So I feel as though I'm changing, I hope I've turned a corner. I can never be too sure, but the signs are incredibly hopeful. I discussed the non-physical relationship I now have with Martha with friends last night and they seemed to understand. It's better for me to live my new life within the realms of realism and accept that I'm never ever going to have her in my life again as a physical human being. So by accepting that and adopting a new 'relationship' with her in this current state, I'm managing my expectations and enjoying what I am able to have with her now.

## Monday 21st October: Day 93

My passport ran out at the end of last year and I've decided to renew it. I don't know when I'll feel able to venture very far, but I'm hopeful. So I'm going to have it there, ready for when that moment arises. It would be truly incredible to go off and have an adventure beyond all this; emotional freedom and self-belief will certainly pave the way for that, but I'll be careful to ensure that enough healing has been done prior to taking the plunge. I thought last night that I'd travel on behalf of Martha and continue to explore as she would certainly have done.

For now I'll stick to exploring this very moment. Every hour of every day I stamp a virtual passport indicating my entry over a brand new border and what an achievement that is. If I close my eyes, I can picture myself by the sea, smelling the breeze and hearing the waves splash. Whenever I do that I can call my girl beside me and smile in the knowledge that my new relationship can make this happen, any time I want.

# Wednesday 30th October: Day 102

Some family and friends stayed over last night as we all need to get up before sunrise this morning to get to Hinksey Lake for the 6.41am start. I didn't sleep too well last night; thoughts of Martha turning sixteen had she still been alive unsettled me.

I check everyone is awake and without thinking ask, "Is Martha up?" I put my hand over my mouth in shock and then laugh – it's not so upsetting now when that happens, it still feels so natural to think about her in the present tense; but I try as much as possible to always use facts rather than let my thoughts lead me into a fantasy world.

As we drive into the city centre it seems busy, even at 6.05am. Numerous groups of cyclists are up and about already, men wearing luminous tabards pass by. There's a crescent moon in the sky, which seems fitting for the day before Hallowe'en. It looks as though it's going to be a lovely day as the sky seems clear. When we arrive at the car park groups of my friends are waiting for us already. It's incredible how many people throughout all this have been so keen and willing to attend any little ritual I suggest in order to help me cope with each milestone. Every single one of them has played a vital part in my recovery.

We walk over to the lake. It feels peaceful here; Martha's friends are by the tree, they don't know I'm coming. I head over to them and say hello. They're so lovely and sweet; I can tell some of them don't know what to say to me so I make it easy for them and chat happily and thank them for coming out so early in the day. We make our way onto the pontoon; there's a mist over the water at the far right corner of the lake, and swans and ducks in the distance.

We organise the tealights to be placed in the water lanterns. I nervously look at my phone to check the time – eight minutes until 6.41am. I take a deep breath and look around; there are about thirty of us standing here quietly watching the day unravel. Two swans swim over to us expecting to be fed; we shine torches on them to try to persuade them to swim away again, but they're undeterred.

Along to my left a friend throws some flower heads into the water and the swans head over to him. He puts his hand out and the swan grabs it, but my friend seems to know what he's doing and doesn't flinch, leaving his hand extended. The swan chomps down in annoyance, but my friend laughs. I look back at my phone to check the time again – one minute to go. I crouch down and gently lift the first lantern; they have square cardboard frames and the main body is made of tissue paper. They're delicate, but hopefully they'll do the job.

At 6.41am, I place the first lantern on the water and gently push it away. It glides out and illuminates the scene with its beautiful, warm amber glow. The swans are curious, but don't seem threatened by this, so I set off the second one. As I do this, friends throw purple, white and sky blue flower heads into the water; it's so peaceful, the water is calm as each lantern is placed, which helps them glide out smoothly. As the sixteenth lantern is placed the current brings all of them back to the edge of the pontoon. We push them along to the right to encourage them to move back out, but the current is against them. We leave them and they eventually make their way out towards the centre of the lake.

At the other side of the lake a passenger train heading to London whizzes past, filled with commuters. What a strange spectacle we must make, standing on a pontoon by a quiet lakeside at this time in the morning. Even stranger is the fact that sixteen years ago today I had a daughter and now I don't. Making something so incredibly unnatural try to seem natural is odd and it makes my head go numb thinking about it. What do I do with all this? I wonder. Where does this take me? Will I get through this with my sanity intact or do I slip gently into a fool's paradise?

Some lanterns gather in groups of two and four as they float further out. They gather and float either side of one of the swans and make for a magical sight. We watch them longingly, our heads filled with our own thoughts. I feel peaceful, tired and slightly nervous about the party later today. I sigh and then suggest that we all head off for breakfast.

We've arranged to go to a local restaurant owned by a friend, who has kindly agreed to open from 7am for us. About twenty or so of us make our way there to find it closed. I've received an ambiguous text from my friend, the restaurant owner, who thinks his staff may have let him down, but he's making his own way in and is only eight minutes away as he's travelling in on his barge to be with us. He's quite eccentric and a bit like an old world explorer, so this doesn't surprise us. Rather than wait out in the cold, some of us head to a local coffee shop to give him time to get his kitchen ready. I feel as though I'm going through the motions of life this morning rather than being in the moment. The early morning start on top of a night of fragmented sleep has left me feeling frayed around the edges and a bit numb.

A friend phones to say that they're ready for us at the restaurant and we all head over. As we arrive there's a buzz of activity. Martha's friend is sorting out the coffee machine, my friends are helping in the kitchen, and my six-year-old cousin has become a mini waiter! It's like a right old family affair – hilariously quirky and patched together. Martha would love this, I think to myself.

We head for home, well-fed but weary. I need to rest and work out a speech for later. I detest public speaking, but need to say something at the beginning of the party to welcome everyone and I'm the only person who can authentically represent Martha. I'm irritable, so I lie on the sofa and rest for half an hour. I'm feeling the pressure of today and although I'm sure the party will be wonderful, it's still a big event to coordinate.

Some friends help my six-year-old cousin carve a pumpkin with stars and a crescent moon to replicate the sky from this morning and we drive it up to Martha's grave. I have a look through the visitors book and note that Martha's friends have been to visit since I was last here. A friend of mine has also brought a tiny pumpkin as a Happy Birthday present; she's inscribed some lovely words onto it and I'm so touched by this thoughtful gesture. I remove any dead flowers and light a candle. I do this without thinking too much. I'm still numb and haven't written my speech yet so we head back home and I start getting myself organised.

I write three paragraphs: a welcome one, one to thank everyone for their support over the past 102 days and one about Martha, who features in the video clip we're starting the party off with. I tweak, scrap and rewrite two more times. I'm happy with the final draft, which is just as well as time is getting on and I need to get showered and ready. I feel the same as I did on the morning of the funeral. The pressure feels immense, but I know that ultimately it'll all work out fine.

Once I'm ready, my lovely cousin does my make-up and then a friend comes to drive me to the venue to start setting up. When we arrive we're met by a team of Martha's friends, who've come along to help. We move tables into diagonal rows, setting chairs around the edges. We've only got enough seats for half the people who are coming, so we need to ensure that most people standing don't impair the view of those sitting down.

The venue is looking great, especially once candles are lit and placed around the room. This lovely, old, majestic building is such a good setting for this event. Formerly St Paul's Church, a Greek revival building designed in 1836, it is now a thriving café-bar. Martha would love this; it's bashed and bruised and unpretentious, which gives it an authentic and relaxed atmosphere.

People start to stream in at 4.20pm, despite the doors not officially opening until 4.30, but this is a good sign. We quickly do the final soundchecks and I try to decide on the final running order with some of Martha's friends who are involved in the proceedings. As some of my friends arrive, they come over to see me, but my head is elsewhere. I politely say hello and suggest they grab a seat quickly as they're limited. I hear my name being called by various people who need me to make some final decisions; I feel anxious and I'm shaking.

I look round and the place has filled up quickly. There are a few faces I don't recognise, so I wander up to introduce myself. One guy turns out to be Martha's kayaking instructor. We talk briefly about how much she enjoyed it; although she never really took it seriously, it got her out of bed early every Saturday to cycle across town to the club and that in itself was a good thing.

As I look around I recognise so many people who make up my life – my entire community is gathered in this lovely building to show their respects. Friends from over the past few decades are all here to support me and to acknowledge how important this day is to me. Many children from Martha's year group were involved and I hope they can also find some peace after today's event.

Before I know it, it's time to get started. The place is packed and people are looking slightly unsure as to what's ahead. Fingers crossed, I hope they enjoy it and that it truly feels like a celebration by the end of it all; I'm feeling very responsible for the emotions of three-hundred people for the next couple of hours.

I've asked a friend to act as compère and explain to everybody what's ahead tonight. He runs the Catweazle Club, which has been going for nearly twenty years and is one of my favourite nights out in Oxford; you never know what you're going to get, but it's always interesting and immensely enjoyable. His expertise is reassuring and you can tell that he's a pro (although his delivery is also soft and toned just perfectly). He introduces me and through the fog of my mind I hear an applause bounding around the building.

I walk up and stand in front of the microphone. I've brought a written note as I'm no good at impromptu public speaking. It all goes OK until half way through someone from the back shouts, "We can't hear you". I shuffle slightly closer to the mic and hear my voice loudly in the speakers to the side of the stage. I don't start from the beginning again as I've already relayed the first two paragraphs, so I just coherently deliver the last paragraph and thank them all for coming.

Funnily enough, the slight malfunction doesn't bother me too much. Who'd criticise me at a time like this? I'm surrounded by compassion and respect, which helps me to brush off things that would have once crushed me in a cascade of self-loathing and disappointment. But these days I'm more confident and pragmatic about things.

I sit down and watch Martha playing the piano piece again. There she is, my girl, safe and well; I take a deep breath: you're OK, I say in my mind. My friend plays the rest of the piece as she did at the funeral party – it works so well. We then show an extended version of a film that contains photos, tweets, video clips of Martha dancing on a school desk – her natural rhythm is evident (I always joke to friends that she got all my rhythm). We finish with a sign saying 'gone to the beach' which is a great way to finish the film off.

The room feels tense; I'm concerned about keeping the right atmosphere considering there are about 130 teenagers in this room – I don't want to break them. Four of Martha's closest friends are sitting one row in front of me; I can see they are clearly emotional after seeing the film. I'm concerned about this as they're about to do their own personal tributes to Martha. They precariously walk up to the mic. It's so brave of them to do this, but you can see that although they're nervous, they're determined to express their thoughts about the dear friend they've lost.

Their words are so adorable and I notice that they speak of her in the present tense. They say that the memories they once thought were insignificant have now become extremely precious. Another recalls how Martha always brought so much food to school as she wanted to put on about two stones – this creates laughter around the room and the atmosphere is lifted slightly, which is a relief. One adds that Martha once said to them "Today is a gift, that's why it's called the present". This well-known phrase, used by my girl, and now used by her friend when remembering Martha, is very touching. I admire these girls so much; they're very young to experience something so distressing, but this is how it is for all of us who've played our part in Martha's life.

We then show a BBC clip from when Martha's school gospel choir was involved in an event called 'Voice in a Million'. Although they're singing 'Joy to the World', Martha looks annoyed. The irony isn't wasted on me – she told me at the time that the teacher made them do a cheesy dance while they sang, which she wasn't happy about. This makes me smile as I watch it again and see her sway from side to side along with the other children. It's good to see her alive and well – even though it's only on a video clip – I can pretend that she's still alive if only for a moment, but I know I mustn't allow myself to do this too much.

Next Martha's friend sings a song called 'Home', by Gabrielle Aplin. Her voice is heavenly and you can tell that people are in admiration of her raw talent and bravery for getting up and doing this in front of such a large group.

I sense a break is needed, so I signal to indicate this and we let the crowd know that we've got a great surprise for them after the break. People get up and head to the bar for drinks and others head for the loos. I'm feeling calmer now, but I'm still shaking. I haven't eaten since breakfast and am too nervous to eat now, which is a shame as we've arranged for pizzas to be delivered throughout the duration of the party from a local pizzeria owned by a friend of mine. His daughter was in Martha's class at primary school and they used to be close friends; it's great to see her here tonight, she's such a lovely girl.

During the break people chat and seem relaxed – there's a lot of positivity and compassion in this room which helps the atmosphere to remain buoyant. I've invited a local reporter and press photographer to feature the party in the local press as I want to ensure that any awareness for future campaigning can be maintained. It's very important to me that people remember how easily Martha's life slipped away and that nobody should close their eyes to what's going on in their own communities.

I feel a great responsibility to play my part in ensuring that future generations are educated fully on the dangers of drugs and I'm also very determined to get involved in schools to ensure this happens. If teenagers are going to dabble, we need to ensure that they are thoroughly educated in order to make informed decisions. So although I'm not condoning drugs, an ongoing dialogue is essential to ensure that necessary changes are made.

I speak to the reporter and hope that I'm properly representing myself. She asks me lots of questions and I have my guard down a bit tonight as I'm distracted by what's going on around me. My focus is off, but I try to relay to her how important it is that we don't jeopardise the possible criminal case that may be ahead of us.

I glance around at the myriad faces. Every few seconds someone comes up to chat to me; they're eager to say the right thing, it's all very polite but genuine. I listen to them and thank them for coming, but my head is struggling as I'm tired and hungry and I'm thinking about what we've got lined up for them next.

The final piece we've planned is a studio-recorded session dedicated to Martha by one of her favourite bands, Little Comets. They're touring around the USA, but very generously agreed to do this for us. I took Martha along with her friend to see them back in 2009 at the O2 in Oxford, when they were the support act for The Noisettes.

They start by saying they're sorry they couldn't attend Martha's event and then begin by singing one of her favourite songs 'Bridge Burn', which also featured in the film we showed earlier. It's an incredible achievement to have managed to pull this off, and is all thanks to one of Martha's friends. If only Martha were here to experience this – a proper 'Super Sweet 16' party for my girl; she'd have gone crazy with excitement I'm sure. She used to watch that TV programme and although I thought it was lavish and gauche, what teenager wouldn't want one?

Next, Little Comets sing 'Jennifer'; the lyrics at the end of this song are 'It was always going to end like this'. Maybe it was, I think to myself, who can know for sure. The grand finale is 'Dancing Song'; the upbeat tempo is a perfect way to end the party so we invite everyone up to dance. Groups of teenagers make their way to the front and start dancing and jumping around – it's great to see them laughing and enjoying themselves.

I feel so strongly for this age group, I feel they don't have a comfortable place in modern society – but thinking back to when I was a teenager I suppose I felt that way too, so perhaps nothing has changed. Perhaps it's an important transitional phase to feel as though you don't fit in and that you need to get to know yourself and work your own way through this period in your life. There is a natural juxtaposition between society and teenagers. I sense that working with teenagers in some capacity in the future may be a good option for me, but we'll see.

A large group then starts doing the 'Cha-Cha Slide' on the stage as they saw Martha dancing to it in one of the video clips we showed earlier. It's a good ice-breaker as I think everyone is a bit drained by the inevitable and underlying sadness of today. They're dancing sequentially and it's funny seeing their individual interpretations. I feel incredibly relieved at how well it's gone and although I'm exhausted, it was worth putting this much effort into today. Keeping busy really helps me to remain motivated and focused, so I'm determined to find a way back – I refuse to be dead as long as I'm still alive.

Some of the children come up to thank me for inviting them and to tell me that they've really enjoyed it. I am so touched by their bravery in coming to talk to me rather than avoiding me, but I also understand when people do that as for some their feelings are too uncomfortable and difficult to contend with.

A handful of friends are still dotted around, so I join them and have my first drink as I'm relaxed now and don't need to remain so focused. We all agree how lovely it was and that it couldn't have gone any better, but I sense we're all feeling that we need to find peace too. Martha is laid to rest and we really did celebrate her life today.

I thank the staff, who've all been exemplary, generous and sensitive. Some friends lovingly help me to gather up the hundreds of condolence cards and gifts I've been given today. I look around once more and the place is almost empty apart from a couple of members of the public who are now settled having a quiet drink – little do they know what just took place in this incredible building. A young and beautiful life was acknowledged and celebrated by so many people who she had a link with. During the 5,742 days, 7 hours and 36 minutes she lived, she reached through to every one of them enough to motivate them to make the effort to come out today and acknowledge the piece in her jigsaw that they represented.

When I will put the final piece of this jigsaw in place is uncertain – it's still too early for that, but the majority of it has been pieced together nicely and paints an incredibly valuable and rich tapestry. Happy sixteenth sweetheart, what a beautiful and interesting girl you were.

# Afterword

I spoke to a friend of Martha about the subject of normal, as I had started refering to my 'new normal'. He very kindly wrote this piece, which he gave me permission to include.

### Normal, by Kanhai Dalal

To put it simply 'normal' is the state in which things usually are. In this particular instance normal would be for Martha to be alive again and living as before. So here I feel it wouldn't be right for us to ever strive for the old state of normal to return. Therefore we must try to create a new normal, in many ways different from the old one, but in many ways similar. This new normal would not entail forgetting Martha and going on with life as it was previously, although for some people less close to her this might be what happens. For me it would mean incorporating her death into how I live, yet moving on and living my own life. What does this mean?

Firstly it *doesn't mean* that by 20th July 2014 everything will be running perfectly; we shouldn't set targets like that. It means that we will have adapted our normal so we can live with the past memories of Martha, while still living in the present and striving for the future.

## Afterword

It feels odd going to rowing and rugby again as if nothing had ever happened. Especially when I'm surrounded by people who weren't as close with Martha and therefore are living life as if almost nothing has happened. To begin with I felt like I wasn't doing Martha justice by carrying on with things, but then I realised I shouldn't feel guilty about carrying on in order to take my mind off things and have fun. She is still in the forefront of my mind and will remain there for some time; however this doesn't mean that I can't have other things going on in my head too.

As much as I don't like it, my new state of normal is starting to form itself. For example, previously when I was free after playing sport I would go straight to Martha's house, stinking like anything, but she didn't mind. I loved going there so much when I was tired after sport because Martha and I would have such simple and innocent fun, which is exactly what you need when you're so tired. So naturally after a tough rowing session last week there was nothing I wanted to do more than to go and spend some time at Martha's house. Then I was hit by the horrible realisation that I couldn't and, more tragically, wouldn't ever be able to do so. On seeing that I looked a bit down my friends took me to the riverside, where we played like little kids in the water and on the bank. Although this fun is very similar to the fun I shared with Martha, it is not a replacement; Martha isn't being replaced by new friends – just as my old normal isn't being replaced by a new one, but is changing. This fact is very difficult for me to accept, but unfortunately it's the truth. I can't try and get back to my old normal; I must adapt it to make my new normal.

# What Martha Did Next

10% of the proceeds from each book sold will be donated to *What Martha Did Next*, a charitable trust which is held and managed by the Oxfordshire Community Foundation CIO Registered Number 1151621.

This fund will be used to facilitate activities to raise awareness of what happened to Martha and to prevent other young people from making the same mistake.

To make a donation or to pledge your support to the work of *What Martha Did Next*, please contact the Oxfordshire Community Foundation on (+44) 01865 798666, email ocf@oxfordshire.org or visit www.justgiving.com/whatmarthadidnext.

| BC | 2/14 |
|----|------|
|    |      |
|    |      |
|    |      |
|    |      |
|    |      |
|    |      |